ETHNIC MILITANCY

AN IRISH CATHOLIC PROTOTYPE

by

James P. Walsh

San Francisco, 1972

Reprinted in 1972 by R and E Research
Associates, publishers and distributors of
ethnic studies. 4843 Mission Street, San
Francisco, California 94112 and 18581 Mc
Farland Avenue, Saratoga, California 95070
Editor: Adam S. Eterovich
Publisher: Robert D. Reed

Library of Congress
Card Catalog No.

72-77022

For

Padraig Breatnac

Ibid., Dec. 8, 1900.

Ibid., Nov. 24, 1900; Dec. 29, 1901; Oct. 6, 1901.

... Dooley, a fictitious Irish saloon-keeper who discussed current affairs with his ... had been created by Finley Peter Dunne in 1893. For more on both see William ... The American Irish (rev. ed., New York: Macmillan, 1966), pp. 145-50.

... Leader, Aug. 2, 1902.

Ibid., Aug. 24; Sept. 7, 1901.

Ibid., Feb. 25, 1905.

Ibid., May 9, 1891.

... Jesse Lemisch, ed., Benjamin Franklin: The Autobiography and Other ... (New York: New American Library, 1961), p. 150.

... Peter C. Yorke, "The Dragon's Teeth," transcript copy, April 23, 1896, ...

... James ... L. M. ... Shaw, A Problem ... instances ... both social and intellectual ... Universal Library ed., New York: Grosset & Dunlap, 1963... pp. 65-74. For ... ... without the benefit of the remarkable volume of literature produced through ... ... in Lincoln and still being produced on this subject.

... Peter C. Yorke, "The Dragon's Teeth," transcript copy, April 23, 1896, p. ... ... Collection, AUSF.

Ibid., p. 39.

Ibid., 13.

Ibid., p. 19.

... Elkins, op. cit. (ref. 6990), [and] Frank Tannenbaum, Slave and Citizen: The Negro ... in ... America (New York: Vintage, 1946), pp. 63-65.

... Hubert Herring, A History of Latin America (2nd ed. rev., New York: Knopf, ... 1961), p. ...

PREFACE

The man around whom this study of ethnic protest has been written is a significant figure in California history. Father Peter C. Yorke in no way dominated state affairs but he was a central figure within his own subculture which, during his lifetime, was a rising, assertive, and highly politicized minority. When Yorke took his seat as a member of the Board of Regents of the University of California he demonstrated how, through direct assault, a militant spokesman of a dissident minority gained access to the decision making body of an allegedly hostile institution.

In the past, historians who have concerned themselves with this man's career have been in agreement on their general interpretation. They have presented Yorke as a social reformer interested in advancing the common good by fighting intolerance and promoting unionization among labor. Also, he has been viewed as an educational reformer. The area of his life into which no writer has probed is his tenure as a Regent of the University of California. This is so even though his Regency was the only aspect of Yorke's life which allowed him the opportunity to step beyond the bounds imposed by his Irish-Catholic-labor milieu.

As both a Regent of the University and an idol of his fellow ethnics, Yorke possessed a truly unique opportunity to facilitate the movement of members of an alienated minority into the mainstream of American intellectual life. He was splendidly located so as to be able to function as a bridge over which the children of his minority group could travel so as to avail themselves of the advantages of higher education.

The first explorations into University of California history were designed simply to discover what Yorke had achieved with his fellow Regents during his tenure. Since earlier writers had characterized him as an educational innovator, expectations were high. The discovery was long in coming but rather clear and unmistakable when it finally emerged. Yorke accomplished nothing of significance. From 1900 to 1912, he became more familiar with the University and the Berkeley community. But as his knowledge increased so did his revulsion.

Yorke's behavior as a Regent is interesting, if somewhat unexpected, and also quite disappointing. This surprising behavior, however, is not understandable without due consideration of his particular personality and temperament, plus his subcultural predispositions -- predispositions he was unable either to control or forget as a Regent. This understanding rests not on the historical composite of Yorke developed by earlier historians, but in part, upon a reinterpretation of their works and on a more wide ranging examination of the environment in which Yorke functioned.

Through the years that Yorke concerned himself with the University, fundamental agreement on basic assumptions was shared by the campus and the dominant sectors of the Berkeley community. By viewing this greater Berkeley consensus against the backdrop of Yorke's world there emerges a study in contrast. The two were diametrically opposed on the issues both judged as vital. Regent Yorke came to recognize the University and its town as alien threats to his own value system. His response, in essence, was one of withdrawal.

That this was not the only mode of behavior possible for an Irish-Catholic Regent was amply demonstrated by a contemporary of Yorke. Garret W. McEnerney, possibly the most valuable Regent the University ever had, shared Yorke's religious affiliations and ethnic background. His response to the University, while quite different, was also fraught with problems. The greater his compatibility with the dominant Berkeley mind, the more he became suspect in the eyes of the working class Irish. This vulnerability reduced his potential influence over his fellow Irish-Catholics and served as the means by which Yorke ultimately rendered him an outcast among his own people.

Father Yorke as a Regent of the University of California is a case history of a unique opportunity lost. The idol of his ethnic community, Yorke in no way used this position to encourage his rising and aggressive young partisans to avail themselves of the benefits of higher education under state auspices. This situation persisted while he officially shared in the direction of the University of California and could assure himself that Irish-Catholic interests were safeguarded.

What follows is not an institutional study which, on occasion, looks out at a fixed world from an internal vantage point. Rather it is essentially an external history of a portion of American life which swirled around, and some of it through, the University of California. Its chapters are not presented here in the order of the author's discoveries. He began by seeking an ethnic militant's achievements. Finding none, he wondered why.

Los Gatos, California
February 18, 1972

TABLE OF CONTENTS

CHAPTER I

PETER C. YORKE: A HISTORICAL PERSPECTIVE

Palm Sunday is a special occasion for the survivors and descendants of San Francisco's onetime Irish-Catholic-labor subculture. In addition to being a day of religious significance for them, it marks also the anniversary of the death of their most fondly remembered public spokesman and champion, Father Peter C. Yorke. For each of the forty-five years since Yorke's death the services conducted in his memory have been a blend of Catholicism, unionism, politics, and Irish nationalism.

The chairman of the annual memorial is always a prominent local Irishman who by then may be past his prime and recognized as an "elder statesman" within Hibernian ranks. Often this person made his name, reputation, and livelihood in city and state politics or in law, vocations both deeply admired and closely related in the subcultural mind. Joining the old man at Yorke's Holy Cross graveside each Palm Sunday are other living symbols of Yorke's lifetime interests and successes. They serve as a link to, and reminder of, a less affluent but more exciting period in the life cycle of the subculture. The pastor of St. Peter's Church represents Yorke's onetime stronghold of Irish-Catholicism in San Francisco. Seated next to him on the speaker's platform is the Irish Consul General, spokesman for his President, Eamon de Valera, the aging revolutionary in whose service Yorke's newspaper was suppressed by the Woodrow Wilson administration.[1] Gratitude for Yorke's noted support during union labor's organizational battles at the century's turn[2] brings the final honored guest to the cemetery. He is a teamster's local president. The priest, the government official, the union executive, all are descendants of those with whom Yorke associated and with whom he comfortably identified.

To refocus attention away from the speaker's stand and on the crowd is to be again struck by continuity and change. The graveside audience is aging and dwindling just as one might expect, in spite of the constant influx of significant Irish immigration. Few under sixty years of age can now remember Yorke, and these only in the recollections of receding youth. Still there is no sign of impending extinction, no suggestion that the yearly pilgrimage be abandoned. Should one converse with individual spectators the most extraordinary revelations concerning Yorke would be encountered. One might indeed be asked if he knew that the reason why Yorke hurried to Rome in 1905 was to head off his jealous bishop's attempts to have him defrocked. Another might let slip that her employer possesses a cache of Yorke's papers, and prizes them so highly that access is denied everyone without exception. One devotee, widely read in Yorke lore is convinced that Yorke always alighned himself on the side of truth, justice, and liberality.

1

To characterize these yearly ceremonies as the devotion of a cult is tempting but also very risky. Many who attend the annual memorial services do so for reasons of sociability and ethnic identity more than because of any affinity of cult. Most never knew Yorke personally. Now having been caught up in the demographic changes associated with middle class status they are dispersed throughout San Francisco and suburbia, often not seeing each other since the last St. Patrick's Day parade. The quantity of oral tradition absorbed by members of this subculture has been limited. Much to the displeasure of memorial speakers, such knowledge has too often been acquired through osmosis while spectators engagingly converse with one another. As the Irish wake is the occasion for sociability and conviviality, even more so is the Yorke re-enactment forty-five years after the fact.

Yorke and His Historians

Even with these considerations in mind the image of Father Yorke has nonetheless taken on rather fixed dimensions. In order to identify these outlines and characteristics with greater exactitude, consultation with the relevant historical literature is required. And the jump from a colorful but inexact oral tradition to recorded "history" is, as will be seen, not all that great.

During his lifetime Peter Yorke was well known as a prominent local figure active in religious and civic affairs. Those who followed his career most closely were his fellow Irish-Catholics. But he was well known beyond this subcultural group, especially among local politicans and union organizers. These latter two, however, were not mutually exclusive of the former category, particularly in San Francisco through the first quarter of the twentiety century. The only activities which brought Yorke beyond the local scene were his work for Irish independence and in the field of education. In both these cases he functioned most often within the confines of the ethnic-religious group with which he identified and from which he drew his sustenance.

Understandably enough then, the significant historical writings relating to Yorke have dealt with Irish-Catholic-labor themes; religious education being the one most frequently treated. Likewise, those who have researched and written to these themes have sprung from this same subculture. The most impressive accomplishments are the Ph.D. disserations of two Catholic priests from The Catholic University of America in Washington, D.C. The first, by Bernard C. Cronin, was published in 1943 as Father Yorke and the Labor Movement in San Francisco, 1900-1910. James P. Gaffey wrote the second, a biography of Yorke's archbishop.

Labor History

Cronin places Yorke within a context of class struggle in San Francisco as the turn of the century.[3] The conflict was two-sided, capital vs labor, with violence a reality and revolution a possibility. Yorke reacted to this configuration of circumstances by devoting himself to the application of Pope Leo XIII's encyclical on the conditions of labor, Rerum Novarum. The motivation for his championship of labor's cause is placed firmly by Cronin within the sphere of religion and morality. Since ". . . deep inner conviction alone could move . . . ."[4] Yorke, he emerges from the labor battles not only as an active social engineer -- a reformer -- but also as an intellectual. This same theme, application of advanced Catholic social theory, is also present in Cronin's article on Yorke in The New Catholic Encyclopedia.[5]

Cronin's monograph is a creditable piece of scholarship, researched and written at a time when those who were associated with Yorke were still living and submitting themselves to interviews by the author. Yorke's associates and confidants have since passed into history themselves, therefore, Cronin's advantage no longer exists to be exploited by subsequent historians.

Church History

Recognizing this handicap, the most recent Yorke scholar, Father James P. Gaffey, plunged deeply into Catholic institutional records of the Archdiocese of San Francisco and Rome. Gaffey's massive and exhaustively researched dissertation, The Life of Patrick William Riordan Second Archbishop of San Francisco, 1841-1914, actually centers on Yorke's first Archbishop.[6] One extensive chapter considers the progressing relationship between the energetic young cleric and his Archbishop. Extracted from the letters and reports which passed between Riordan's Chancery and his religious superiors in Rome is a view or evaluation of Father Yorke not available to the public domain until Gaffey's research. In 1893 at age twenty-nine, two years after the completion of his graduate studies, the youthful curate was chosen by his Archbishop to serve as the Chancellor of the Archdiocese and as his secretary. Such selections in the normal course of events were interpreted as indicators of higher honors in the future. From such selections are the upper echelons of the Church's hierarchy ultimately staffed.

Before death overtook Riordan, Yorke's relationship with him deteriorated from initial cooperation, to conflict, and came to rest in coexistence. Rome first heard of Father Yorke in 1896 when bishops from the Northwest forwarded his name for Rome's consideration. A Washington fishop had died and his see was to be filled. Riordan's contemporary view was that at the moment, Yorke was "little more than a boy to whom it would be dangerous to give the care of a diocese."[7] Even though he was very much attached to the highly personable young priest, Riordan felt, at that time, that prudence required he be given ten more years of experience so his sense of judgement might mature.

By 1901 Yorke was so well known as a public champion of his church in the West that he became a source of some embarrassment within the hierarchy. So prominent was Yorke that when a list of three was sent to Rome for the selection of a bishop for Cheyenne, the omission of his name was a cause for explanation. "Although brilliant and eloquent . . . he is so offensive to . . . the Most Reverend Archbishop of San Francisco, that he cannot be proposed by us."[8]

The following year Archbishop Riordan sought to negotiate with Rome for a coadjutor to assist him in San Francisco, one who would have the right to succeed him upon his death. The normal procedure on such occasions was for the bishops to consult among the local clergy and form a list of three to be sent to Rome. The vote following consultation tied Yorke for second place with two others. Even though one of the others declined to be included, Yorke nonetheless was removed from the Terna. This final list was accompanied by an explanation of Yorke's unfitness for the hierarchy and an unanimous recommendation that he never be elevated to the rank of bishop.[9]

Gaffey's research was an institutional study, and it was he who, for the first time, revealed the official views toward Yorke of those who held power within the local Catholic Church. These evaluations determined his official place within the formal institution but not in the emotions of the Irish sector of San Francisco's population. Certainly most of those who share in the oral tradition kept alive through Palm Sunday memorials would reject the formal evaluations were they knowledgeable of them.

Certain characteristics attributable to Yorke as he appears in Gaffey's work can be agreed upon by all; by his clerical superiors, the Irish-Catholic subculture then and now, and by those who have written of him. He was a man of ability, zeal, and devotion who defended his religious faith pungently, both in the press and on the stage against unsympathetic antagonists. Most would also agree that purdence was not Yorke's outstanding characteristic. On this point interpretations divide. Yorke's Archbishop placed greater weight on prudent behavior than did the mass of his predominantly working class flock. He felt in time that this lack of prudence was a risk to their institution, particularly so in Yorke's case, because his narcissistic ego propelled him into situations that less perceptive and less talented men would pass by. From the vantage point of the administrator, the keeper of institutions, Yorke was not only unpredictable and therefore unsafe but also an "ingrate" to his spiritual father, Archbishop Riordan.[10]

Gaffey did not concern himself with Yorke's activity in the labor movement but accepts Cronin's work as given. Because of the scope of that topic, the nature of the sources, and the quality of Cronin's monograph, it is unlikely than in independent exploration will or even should be attempted. Instead Gaffey charted the deterioration of Yorke's relationship with his Archbishop over the backdrop of anti-Catholic nativism, which came to full bloom nationally in the 1890's.[11] The local manifestation of this phenomenon took the form of the American Protective Association, and by meeting the thrusts of this nativism, Father Yorke first attracted public notice.

Social History

A high degree of agreement exists between Gaffey's interpretation of Yorke vs the A.P.A. and the one advanced earlier by two independent authors,[12] David J. Herlihy in "Battle Against Bigotry" and Joseph S. Brusher, S.J., in "Peter C. Yorke and the A.P.A. in San Francisco." These two agree that the American Protective Association represented a serious threat to the well-being of the Catholic Church in San Francisco. Bogus patriots, the A.P.A. represented the forces of intolerance, bigotry and paranoia, which sought to undermine the religious convictions of Catholics along with their socio-economic position and their political rights. San Francisco nativism burst into flames at this time because of a combination of factors. The latent suspicion many

Americans harbored for the Catholic Church had been fanned by Frank Pixley, editor of the San Francisco Argonaut, since the 1870's.[13] Foreign immigration and the polyglot condition of San Francisco set the stage for religious antagonism[14] -- antagonism which erupted with the complaints of the growing Catholic population over the use of a public school history book which they judged biased against their religion.

Each writer generally agreed in interpretation. The A.P.A. provoked ". . . the rise of one of the Church's most brilliant and irrepressible defenders, Father Peter C. Yorke."[15] "This young priest bore single-handed the brunt of the A.P.A. attacks . . ., met and routed their champions in controversy, and ruthlessly tore the veil from the devious methods by which these 'patriots' strove to protect America."[16]

"Yorke," we are told, "made men proud to be Catholics." If A.P.A. types damaged the Catholic champion, it was no more than making him "too violent in the defense of justice, too reckless in the support of truth."[17]

The heart of the great controversy touched on anti-popery-type sermons delivered as Sunday afternoon lectures by denominational ministers, which in turn were given full press coverage in the dailies the following Monday. Yorke responded first in the Catholic paper, The Monitor which he edited, later in the city dailies and on the lecture circuit. He found himself in a position similar to the political candidate whose opponent was spreading vicious lies about him. One alternative was to preserve one's dignity by ignoring the libel and hoping to be recognized as a person of quality who has risen above the squalor. A second alternative was to recognize the slur, demonstrate its fallaciousness and inquire into the nature of persons who could possibly purvey such vileness. Yorke chose the latter and drove the war into his enemy's camp by inflitrating their organization, carrying on lengthy press battles with A.P.A. writers and challenging their speakers to open debate with a purse going to the winner. He had a sense of the dramatic and knew how to please the crowd. In the end Yorke bested his antagonists in the war of words. A.P.A. political candidates failed in attempts at public office and A.P.A. support ceased being respectable or fashionable in San Francisco.

The writings of Herlihy, Brusher and Gaffey tend to interpret Yorke's successful tilt with the San Francisco A.P.A. as a triumph of truth, justice, toleration, and liberality over the forces of bigotry, provincial narrowness, and ignorance. Yorke appears as a champion of principle, of abstract good.

At the end of his chapter on Yorke and nativism, Gaffey hints that both Yorke and his Archbishop lacked adequate balance. Riordan administered his diocese with the efficiency of a smoothly run business operation but was an inadequate leader because he remained silent on the social and economic issues of the day. He gave no guidance to his flock who looked to him for it. Like the Tammany Irish who ran New York City government for seventy years, he acted as if society were static and once he had power he did not use it for social purposes.[18]

Riordan drew on the obvious talents of Yorke, once he had decided the time for ignoring the A.P.A. had passed and the time for counterattack had begun. He called

Yorke to active duty and sustained him in combat as long as Yorke's behavior, in Riordan's judgement, served the institution. Once it ceased to serve what the Archbishop considered the good of the Church, once Yorke became elevated by the roar of the crowd and began indulging his ego, then Riordan withdrew his official support and cut Yorke off from ecclesiastical preferment.

Following such treatment from Riordan, Yorke became even less restrained by institutional inhibitions. He was cut off from the concerns of the Chancery and not only did not care about prudence in decision making, he no longer was officially knowledgeable as to what the current decisions involved. Instead Yorke used his power, based on widespread popularity within the Irish-Catholic-labor subculture, for social engineering. He was committed to principle. He was a reformer.

His popular support within his own subculture is easy to understand. At the turn of the century this subculture was predominantly working class, Irish, and Catholic. Members felt put-upon by those in the more elevated strata of socio-economic life who did not share their own religious affiliations. Yorke was undeniably one of their own and they gloried in his attack on employers and religious bigots. They liked his style. He was a fighter and they could vicariously share in his victories over the respectables.

Yorke as an Orator

Not only could he trade body blows with bigots and flay fellow Celts with barnyard Gaelic when he considered them renegades to the Irish working class, but he could always rise to eloquence in flawless English speech when the occasion demanded. Popular mythology suggests that every Irishman is an orator, the myth being cultivated by the speeches of an inordinate number of Irish rebels delivered on the eve of execution. In America the myth took on the qualities associated with urban politics, as symbolized in the style of Bourke Cockran, the old-time Tammany spellbinder who first placed Al Smith's name in nomination before the 1920 Democratic Convention.

What one person considers eloquent another does not. If beauty is in the eye of the beholder, then eloquence might be conditioned by the shared emotional and psychological experiences of the auditors. If this be so, Yorke had a splendid advantage in that his followers shared the same cultural experiences, and to this homogeneous audience he brought undeniable oratorical talents. A perceptive evaluation of "Father Yorke in the Pulpit,"[19] appeared the year his collected works were published, 1931. Brother Leo of St. Mary's College, Yorke's oratorical understudy judged his idol

> . . . a controversialist stingingly and effectively superb; . . . a master
> of English, pellucid, nervous, eloquent. He was a devastating satirist
> and a humorist irresistible and contagious . . . . Those of us who grew
> up in the community which he adorned can never be persuaded that the
> age of our youth was not a golden age indeed.[20]

In classifying Yorke's oratorical style for pedagogical purposes, Brother Leo labeled it the "Irish mode," a distinctive use of English favored by Irish writers who crystalized, in what he considered flawless speech, the experiences of their shared ethnic and emotional backgrounds.[21] Quite obviously all Irishmen are not eloquent. Like other ethnic groups they have their share of the inarticulate. The Irish-Catholic-labor subculture did consider Yorke eloquent though, because Yorke's gift for words articulated their felt but unexpressed emotions.

Brother Leo gave what he considered an example of Yorke's eloquence, a view that would be agreed to by those who shared a cultural identity, those who had not yet sunk their roots deeply enough into the California soil to feel secure and at ease.

Recalling to mind years later than when Yorke spoke at the funeral of a St. Mary's brother in 1902, "eyes dimmed and lips quivered and shoulders shook . . . ."[22] Turning to the black robes who remained Yorke continued:

> And you, his brothers in the Christian schools, you have in his life and memory a model of your estate. As one said who knew him well: "He was every inch a Christian Brother." He loved you and he was loyal to you . . . . Bear him forth tenderly to his long home and his last restingplace, for he has earned home and rest. No more in life will you behold his kindly presence or listen to his welcome voice. But he had only gone before you. Pray that it may be well with him today in the sight of God, when the judgment sits and the books are opened.

> And now, dear friend of me and mine, it is time to say good-bye. Thou shalt lie far from Glenanar and the lordly Shannon and the city's towers and the fair hills of holy Ireland. But thy grave shall be also a holy place in this new and beautiful land to which thou didst give thy life and thy labors, and a spot of benediction among this people whom thou didst love. No man of thy blood or clan may ever kneel by thy resting-place to say a prayer for thy soul, but thou shalt not be forgotten. Thy spiritual children will come -- they and their sons after them -- to thank God at thy grave that thou wast given unto them a teacher and a friend.[23]

Yorke as an Educator

Yorke's activity in the field of education is the topic treated by the remaining available historians. Their works include three master's degree theses, one each from The Catholic University of America, Domincan College in San Rafael, California, and The University of San Francisco.[24] Added to these is the most recently published article on Yorke, appearing in The Catholic Educational Review.[25]

All agree on the importance of Yorke's educational work and its influence on Catholic education in the United States. When he entered the scene, the sisters in the local Catholic schools were struggling in their attempts at religious education. Their text, the Baltimore Catechism, had been mandated by the Third Plenary Council of Baltimore, 1884, and they were no more pleased with its selection than classroom teachers today having to comply with similar mandates. Yorke came to their rescue by publishing a series of Text Books of Religion. In consultation with the teachers and after pilot classroom use, he provided for the grading of the Catechism's content, its integration with scripture and the Catholic liturgy. He topped it off with the inclusion of elementary visual aids.[26]

As a leader and officer in the National Catholic Educational Association, Yorke guided the destinies of that group and introduced and explained its work to the Catholic people.[27] As a priest looked upon as knowledgeable on educational subjects, he was called often to express his views. In general terms he advocated standardization, rationalization and greater professionalization within the Catholic schools. He put forth an admirable method for lesson planning which included a cross disciplinary approach to the topic being considered, consideration of learning theory, evaluation of instruction and reorganization for more successful learning on future occasions. He strongly recommended that in addition to fulfilling each of the steps in his comprehensive plan, the entire package must be prayed over, and with fervor.[28]

Religion, according to Yorke, was the chief factor in education, and education without it was so dangerous that Christian children might be better off with no education.[29] To be a successful teacher one needed solid subject matter preparation which first required courses that somehow trained the mind in habits of clear and precise thinking, and only after these should specialized and professional courses be attempted.[30] But Yorke ". . . always maintained the superiority of the spiritual formation of the teacher over any professional training."[31]

Father Brusher seems to reflect the interpretation of the other writers in labeling Yorke an educator who transcended the limitations of his own time. Out of these writings the Yorke of history appears with added attributes; a deep sense of historical perspective, sturdy common sense, dedication, broadness of vision and billiance. In fact, Yorke is placed in the same category as John Henry Newman, both recipients of the degree Laurea Nomine Sanctae Sedis, both outstanding Catholic intellectuals.[32] The consensus seems to be that although Yorke was active throughout his life in a great many fields, his most effective influence probably was as an educator,[33] and it is in his educational work where the essence of the man is to be found.[34] Since "the boundaries of Father Yorke's vision were the boundaries of the world,"[35] his educational achievements were not circumscribed by narrow sectarian lines. As a Regent of the University of California for ten years

> . . . he studied and helped solve the various problems facing the administration of the State University. During this time he gave much of his attention to the development of the California educational system. He could be just as interested and work just as hard in any field of endeavor, among all men, regardless of race or creed.[36]

The Historical Composite

The composite Yorke arising out of history seems at this point a truly remarkable human being. Those who were close to him and knew him well found him a highly personable, warm human being. He was engaging as a conversationalist and eloquent as an orator. He was a man of ability, zeal, and devotion whose tendency toward imprudence brought him into conflict with his Archbishop. Those who approve of this might interpret the data as demonstrating his independence and sense of liberation from hierarchical authority, while those who disapprove might call it insubordination of self-seeking. Yorke was an irrepressible defender and advocate of religious liberty. In fact he was an activist-reformer, a social engineer who stood above special interest in his advocacy of principle and abstract good. In education he was in advance of his time as a pedagogue, and as a Regent of the University of California displayed the breadth of vision which liberated him from the charge he was interested in his sect alone. He was a broad-minded intellectual and a brilliant one.

This general image of Father Peter C. Yorke has been compiled by eight writers in works of varying magnitude. The Yorke of these dimensions has sprung from examinations of his conflict with the American Protective Association, his assistance of union labor in the organizational battles of the early century, and his work in the field of education. In succeeding chapters the first of these will be re-examined, the second will be re-interpreted, and the third will be re-explored from a new vantage point.

[1] *The Leader*, July 19, 1941.

[2] Bernard C. Cronin, *Father Yorke and the Labor Movement in San Francisco, 1900-1910* (Washington D.C.: Catholic University of America, 1943).

[3] Ibid., p.14.

[4] Ibid., p.22.

[5] B. C. Cronin, "Yorke, Peter Christopher," *New Catholic Encyclopedia,* XIV (New York: McGraw-Hill, 1967), p.1075.

[6] James P. Gaffey, *The Life of Patrick William Riordan: Second Archbishop of San Francisco, 1841-1914* (Ph.D. dissertation, Catholic University of America, 1965).

[7] Ibid., p.399.

[8] Ibid., p.416.

[9] Ibid., pp. 417-8.

[10] Ibid., p.421.

[11] For background to this manifestation of American nativism see Ray Allen Billington, *The Protestant Crusade, 1800-1860* (Chicago: Quadrangle, 1964). The story is continued through the period being considered here by John Higham, *Strangers in the Land: Patterns of American Nativism, 1860-1925* (New York: Atheneum, 1965).

[12] David J. Herlihy, "Battle Against Bigotry: Father Peter C. Yorke and the American Protective Association in San Francisco. 1893-1897," *Records of the American Catholic Historical Society of Philadelphia*, IXII (June, 1951); Joseph S. Brusher, S.J., "Peter C. Yorke and the A.P.A. in San Francisco," *The Catholic Historical Review*, XXXVII (July, 1951).

[13] Herlihy, op.cit., p.99.

[14] Gaffey, op.cit., p.362.

[15]Ibid., p. 361.

[16]Brusher, op. cit., p. 130.

[17]Herlihy, op. cit., p. 120.

[18]Daniel B. Moynihan, "When the Irish Ran New York," The Reporter, 24 (June 8, 1961), 32-34.

[19]Brother Leo, "Father Yorke in the Pulpit," The Moraga Quarterly, II (Fall, 1931), 30-40.

[20]Ibld., p. 31.

[21]Ibid., p. 37.

[22]Ibid., p. 39.

[23]P. C. Yorke, Sermons (San Francisco: Text Book Publishing, 1931), I, 322-3.

[24]James H. Long, A Factual Study of the Influence of Reverent P. C. Yorke on Education (M. A. thesis, Catholic University of America, 1932); Sister Mary C. Manion Principles of Catechetical Instruction According to Reverend Peter C. Yorke (M. A. thesis, Domincan College, 1953); Sister Mary C. Fitzmaurice, B. V. M., Historical Development of the Educational Thought of the Reverend Peter C. Yorke, 1893-1925 (M. A. thesis, University of San Francisco, 1963).

[25]Joseph S. Brusher, S. J., "Peter C. Yorke, Educator Ahead of His Time," The Catholic Educational Review, XLIV (Feb., 1966).

[26]Ibid., p. 110-5; Long, op. cit., p. 29.

[27]Fitzmaurice, op. cit., p. 100.

[28]Manion, op. cit., p. 45-6.

[29]Ibid., p. 33; Fitzmaurice, op. cit., p. 35.

[30]Long, op. cit., p. 33-4.

[31]Manion, op. cit., p. 47.

[32]Joseph S. Brusher, S.J., "Peter C. Yorke, Educator Ahead of His Time," The Catholic Educational Review, XLIV (Feb., 1966), 115.

[33]Ibid., p. 106.

[34]Fitzmaurice, op. cit., p. 114.

[35]Ibid., p. 80.

[36]Ibid., p. 10.

CHAPTER II

A RECONSIDERATION OF THE MAN

Irish Origins

The environment out of which Peter Yorke sprang was one thoroughly understood, if not actually shared, by the core of San Francisco's Catholic community through more than the first quarter of the twentieth century. Like almost all the contemporary clergy in the Archdiocese, Yorke was not American born but from Ireland.[1] But unlike most of his fellow Irish Catholics in America, his origins were not connected with the village or a small potato farm. He was a city lad born in Galway in 1864. Galway was the primary commercial town in the West of Ireland, a market place for fishermen and the farmers who tilled the rocky soil of beautiful but desolate Connemara. Galway's market places undoubtedly rang with the sound of Gaelic, as the West was then a region where the native language flourished. Yorke himself was a native Gaelic speaker and waged a lifelong battle against the trend toward its extinction. Yorke spent his youth in the only town of size in the West, where because of foreign rule his religion and nationality were not reasons for preference within the political, economic, and social institutions of the day.

Yorke carried with him through life the cultural baggage accumulated in the Ireland of his youth. And as the end approached, he thought not of the new American life that had opened for himself and for those who shared his culture but rather his reverie returned him to the Ireland of 1886, the year he departed for the New World. In his diary jottings, he seems to have calculated the subsequent thirty-eight years as time spent in exile.[2]

Education consumed the great part of Yorke's first twenty-two years in Ireland. At the early age of eleven he ceased attending the local Galway schools and began to study for the priesthood in the provincial town of Tuam, also in County Galway. At age eighteen he matriculated to St. Patrick's College in Maynooth. During his four years of study at the national seminary he displayed above average scholastic ability. The last two years of his preparation for the priesthood were completed in Baltimore, Maryland, at St. Mary's Seminary where he was ordained by James Cardinal Gibbons, in December of 1887. By this time his mother had emigrated from Galway and was settled in Hayward, California.

Through mutual agreement Yorke had been adopted by the Archdiocese of San Francisco and had completed his training under its auspices, a procedure which then was not uncommon since Ireland produced priests in superabundance while much of its population was America bound. The clergy of American birth had long since been overrun by Catholic immigrants. The adoption of Irish seminarians was a natural and popular alternative, one chosen by San Francisco's Archbishop.[3] Had the old American church dating back to John Carroll of Maryland a choice in the matter, slower and more orderly growth would have been preferred.[4] But since the Irish famine years particularly, no such option existed. In time of course, this practice resulted in exclusive Irish control of the Church in more urbanized areas. By the year of Yorke's death one estimate put the Irish born clergy in the San Francisco Archdiocese at seventy-five percent of the total.[5] In Riordan's last report to Rome he stated that of his eighty-eight priests sixty-four were Irish born. Only four were Americans by birth.[6] And of those who were born in America the largest block were of Irish parentage. This trend existed before Yorke's arrival and continued 'til past his death. In this set of circumstances he found a comfortable niche.

Yorke and the A.P.A.: A War of the Godly

Two years after the completion of graduate studies at the newly established Catholic University of America Yorke, aged twenty-nine, became the Chancellor of the Archdiocese of San Francisco and secretary to his Archbishop. The following year, 1894, Riordan appointed him Editor-in-Chief of the official Catholic newspaper, The Monitor.[7] From this post the young priest challenged the American Protective Association in San Francisco. As a result of his role in the A.P.A. controversy, he loomed large in the popular mind of his subculture, and in subsequent local history he has become larger than the threatening and dangerous monster he met and destroyed.

The phenomenon of American nativism has been exceedingly well covered as a significant factor in our national history, the twin thrusts being xenophobia and anti-Catholicism.[8] To apply what is taken as a national synthesis to a local community would appear to be a questionable practice, however, from the methodological vantage point. While there may be greater justification for interpreting national history as a synthesis resting on a homogenization of local and regional circumstances, the reverse procedure is at best fraught with serious risk. In the case of San Francisco the risk could be especially perilous in that from its beginning this city has been hardly representative of the nation at large, particularly those parts in which fundamental nativism flourished best. At first glance one might wonder how xenophobia could even exist in such a cosmopolitan setting where over a third of the 1900 population was foreign born,[9] and the aggregate of persons with at least one foreign born parent approached the total population.[10]

In spite of this there were manifestations of A.P.A. type sentiment in San Francisco before the century's turn. The public spokesmen of the A.P.A. Councils have been identified as denominational preachers who spent their Sunday's fuming over Romish plots against America.[11] These gentlemen received liberal publicity since their lectures were well covered by the press, as were other sparse weekend news events. Oratory at the Council meeting also acquired an ominous ring as the locals pledged to live up to their national oath,[12] which forbade economic intercourse with Catholics when at all possible. In this spirit the superintendent of the Union Iron Works announced he would not employ a Catholic when he could obtain the services of a Protestant.[13]

Those writers who have dealt with the A.P.A. in San Francisco have focused on the ministers who gave public expression to the nativist thrust. Beyond this the content of the Councils and the socio-economic identity of the nativists remains largely in the shadows. Nasty oratory and its equivalent in the press are the point of focus. The presumed grass roots support which supposedly made the A.P.A. an economic, social, political and religious threat to Catholics takes on shadowy characteristics. It assumes these attributes because, first, it is presumed evil, and second, since it is unknown in magnitude it must be powerful. When this evil colossus is met and defeated, Yorke emerges greater than the monster he slew. Unfortunately the only measure of A.P.A. strength systematically applied has been restricted to the quality and quantity of its oratory. Popular support for San Francisco's nativist binge has not been calculated by any quantitative method.

As those who deal with social phenomena well know, there is a very large drop-off from the expression of an opinion to action on that opinion, from disapproval of a policy, to writing to a Congressman, to contributing money, to relinquishing all gainful employment to become a volunteer reformer. If one could judge from conclusions drawn from the accompanying population data, San Francisco was unfertile ground indeed for any nativist thrust of a substantial popular base. Rather than the phenomenon running deep into American national life and reflecting wide, local support the fumings of the San Francisco ministers and an occasional "industrialist" at the superintendent's level might more logically signify nothing beyond what they were -- talk, heated to be sure, but still talk, restricted to a minority sector of the population of a large cosmopolitan community.

San Francisco in 1900 was a city characterized by ethnic diversity. The two largest identifiable groups were German and Irish, with 101,000 and 95,000 respectively.[14] A very distant third were the English with 35,000, just a bit better than one third of the German total. Were one roughly to calculate the aggregate of immigrants and their children from which might likely be drawn active adversaries on the issue of popery, the Pope might indeed have prevailed. Because of the difficulty in determining which Germans were Protestants and which ones were Catholics, this bloc ought probably to be omitted from the calculations. In any case it seems unlikely that the actual division could have favored Protestants by better than four to one -- the ratio needed to tip the one-sided balance. Also, when you consider the transition from the potency of raw numbers to political and economic activity, the Germans, whether Protestant or Catholic, did not possess the advantage of linguistic compatibility as did the Irish. All the Irish spoke English, even those from the old country -- the few Gaelic speakers being bilingual. Over a third of the Germans in San Francisco were foreign born. Their linguistic compatibility there fore was less. Undoubtedly some of the San Francisco Irish were from what later became the North of Ireland and sympathized with the A.P.A. Their numbers must have been few, for when Riordan named his new seminary he stated it was because St. Patrick was:

> The patron . . . of a great Catholic race to which the vast majority of
> our people belong . . . the most devoted, the most generous, the most
> priest loving race within the fold of the Church of Christ.[15]

San Francisco Population, 1900

by Ethnic Background

		Catholic tendency	anti-Catholic tendency
Austria	5,499	X	
Australia	1,096		
Belgium	291*	X	
Canada (English)	14,168		X
Canada (French)	1,716	X	
China	10,762*		
Denmark	6,469		X
England	34,760		X
Finland	935*		
France	15,437	X	
Germany	100,718		
Holland	244*		
Hungary	987		
Ireland	94,782	X	
Italy	22,986	X	
Japan	1,852*		
Mexico	1,459	X	
Norway	5,879		X
Poland	2,930	X	
Portugal	530*		
Russia	4,650		
Scotland	13,116		X
South America	370*	X	
Spain	235*		
Sweden	14,197		X
Switzerland	6,458		
Wales	1,652		X
		145,470	90,241

---

*Foreign born only and not their children. Except where indicated, the above numbers refer to San Franciscans of foreign birth and those with at least one foreign parent. The total population of San Francisco in 1900 was 342,782. Of these only 84,998 were of native parents. The above data were compiled from United States Census Office, Twelfth Census of the United States, 1900 (Washington: 1901), I, 738-9, 868, 876-7, 884-5, 892-3, 900-1, 904-5.

These Irish, about whom their Archbishop spoke so fondly, were the second largest ethnic group in the city, had the advantage of linguistic compatibility over the largest block, the Germans, and drew off an unknown amount of German support through their own dominance within the Catholic Church. In addition to this it should be noted that while the total Irish and German populations were not so far apart in total numbers, over twice as many Germans were from the old country as compared with the Irish. If you consider only American born members of the respective ethnic communities, the Irish were considerable ahead (13,000+). Presumably the added generation in America turned the foreigner into a marginal man,[16] which enabled him to better manipulate the American environment while still understanding through experience the needs of the foreign born.

American Born Irish and Germans

San Francisco, 1900

	Irish	German
Total	94,782	100,718
Foreign Born	15,963	35,194
American Born	78,819	65,524
	65,524	
	13,295 (Irish plurality)	

The Irish have been correctly identified as the core of the Catholic Church. In San Francisco their Archbishop attested to the fact locally. While not quite true in all cases, Irish was roughly equivalent to Catholic in San Francisco. Unfortunately for present purposes no such easy equivalent existed to link other sizable ethnic groups to binding religious affiliations.

The use of general California population data must be considered with extreme caution since San Francisco has never been representative of the state. To cite such general data as relevant to the San Francisco situation is in fact perilous since the two great population centers of the state were quite divergent. Los Angeles was filling up with Mid-Westerners inclined toward populism, Protestant morality, and later toward Progressivism. San Francisco was heavily Catholic, ethnic, less strict on moral issues, and less willing to experiment in the political sphere. The state was by 1900 very heterogeneous.[17]

In dealing with Yorke and his A.P.A. battle, Father Gaffey applied to San Francisco the population statistics of the state in general as used in another work.[18] Through the decade of the 1880's new immigration intensified the Protestant magnitude but by 1906 California Catholics still made up 58 percent of the state's churchgoing population.[19] This figure has little relevance as far as Yorke and the A.P.A. are concerned. Theirs was a local and not a state wide controversy. More to the point would be the relative distribution of churchgoing San Franciscans. The population of the city at the turn of the century was slightly less than 350,00, and of these, 143,000 were churchgoers.

Unbelievable as it may seem 116,000 were Roman Catholics while only 22,000 were Protestants of all denominations. In Los Angeles where the population was just about half that of San Francisco, general church attendance approached equality, with Protestant bodies exceeding the Roman Catholics by a significant margin (70,000 to 52,000).[20]

Two conclusions emanate from this examination of the statistics. First, state wide figures have no meaning for San Francisco. Second, and much more important, if the heart of the A.P.A. was certain ministers in certain Protestant churches, what serious religious, political, and economic threat could they be to Yorke's Catholic community when the totality of active Protestants in San Francisco were, by the nearest available data, outnumbered by over five to one? Given the nativist feelings of this mini-minority, it would seem more appropriate to interpret their incendiary oratory not as the signal for anti-Catholic action, but rather as no more than the steam being emitted from the safety valve of men's minds when they found themselves unable to take significant action on beliefs they considered so true.

The most specific example cited of economic action against San Francisco Catholics -- the Union Iron Works superintendent -- was, as far as we know, no action at all. It was more oratory. The fact that this industry at the turn of the century ran an advertisement in Catholic parish picnic programs might lead to the conclusion the superintendent's talk had no lasting effect in the realm of action.[21] If the superintendent reflected company policy, it is unlikely such advertisements, or really contributions, would later have been considered. Yorke delighted friends and outraged foes, but made few converts.

Herlihy, like Gaffey, rather than going to the official population statistics specific to San Francisco cites the same secondary source for state wide data.[22] According to Herlihy the yeomanry of the A.P.A. was not made up of native Americans after all, but rather Scandinavians, Canadians, and Orangemen who were strongly anti-Catholic from the start.[23] If these groups could perform the gymnastics required in order to consider themselves honorary native Americans, a feat which would allow them to abuse other foreigners and in itself be compatible with the dominant culture in their new country, what actual power did they have over their antagonists? As recent immigrants themselves they presumably were not yet in key or decision making posts in the economic or political life of the city. Like other recent arrivals they competed in the market place only with force of numbers and even here the Catholic Irish alone had them badly outnumbered.

An examination of the ethnic composition of San Francisco displays, then, that in a popular contest between immigrant and native sectors of the community, the balance would go to the immigrant.[24] Within the immigrant sector the subtotal of those who might consider themselves honorary natives out to save America from the foreign menace of Rome is not sufficiently large. Less likely also would be the possibility that individuals from this minority would be in positions to act on their convictions.

Through the literature dealing with Yorke and the A.P.A. runs two standards by which the nativists were measured. The first, oratorical bombast, has already been considered. The A.P.A. was presumed a threat because of what its spokesmen said. The measure of its strength was the virility of its oratory. The decline of the A.P.A. was marked by successive ministers retiring from the press war with Yorke, at least one of them leaving town. The results of the municipal election of 1896, however, are presented as the coup de grace,[25] the final victory signal for Yorke and the principle of tolerance.[26] In this local election James D. Phelan, a San Francisco born Irish-Catholic and future United States Senator, was elected Mayor over the A.P.A. backed candidate. Two different standards then have been applied to the A.P.A. Its strength rested on the volume of its oratory which spilled over into newsprint. Its fall was marked by a political criterion.

An appropriate question, which never seems to have been asked, is: Why should one believe that the A.P.A. in San Francisco had any political strength in the first place? With San Francisco's ethnic content, endorsement by a nativist group could be the politician's kiss of death. Repudiation of such support could endear a candidate to victims of injustice who at the same time conveniently happened to represent a huge majority of the electorate.

Voting theory rests on certain assumptions and empirical data. Key among these is that people vote for their interest and not against it. On the political horizon there are certain bench marks used by voters to orient themselves. If they are positively oriented toward one of these and the guide favors candidate "A", then those voters will vote for "A" also. The reverse would be true if their orientation were negative or if their point of political orientation opposed "A". And also, when a clearly recognizable member of an ethnic minority heads a ticket, the vote of that ethnic bloc goes to that candidate and his ticket.[27] It might be added that a reasonable extension would suggest that voters of different ethnic backgrounds would be strongly inclined to vote for an ethnic candidate particularly when he shared their religion which was under attack by supporters of his opponent.

In light of these newly developed data and currently accepted voting theory, Yorke's role in the A.P.A. controversy, the controversy which gave him his power, reputation, and following in the Irish-Catholic-labor subculture of San Francisco, needs to be re-interpreted. All that has been demonstrated to now concerning the A.P.A. in San Francisco is that some of its local spokesmen said vile things about the Catholic Church, things that offended many San Franciscans, most of them being Catholics. An objective fact, never stressed by Yorke's interpreters, is that the A.P.A. organization never held political power. Also, if it possessed any economic power, its magnitude was unknown. If it existed at all, it has been unexplored.

Yorke did a splendid job in quieting the claptrap emanating from lecture platforms and the press. This achievement took talent, courage and hard work. By poking fun at the bigot and by routing him from the city, Yorke elevated the drooping morale of a newly arrived working class that had an international history of abuse. To claim that he saved the bread-winner's job and voting rights from the clutches of the A.P.A. seems, however, an overstatement. His lectures in 1896 may indeed have brought out the vote but few opinions could have been changed.

The A.P.A. conflict in San Francisco was a war of the godly and seems to have had few ramifications beyond the confines of the participants' own minds, other than reinforcing the political inclinations that already existed in a city of great ethnic diversity. If Yorke's stature rests on the objective strength of the American Protective Association which he silenced in San Francisco, it rests on little more than a loud and troublesom phantom, but a phantom, nonetheless.

Yorke and Labor: Reformer or Partisan Leader?

Briefly let us consider Yorke's role as a supporter of organized labor in San Francisco. The place to begin would seem to be the Cronin monograph, Father Yorke and the Labor Movement in San Francisco 1900-1910. As has been noted elsewhere, this scholarly work sets the stage with San Francisco in the grip of class conflict, capital vs. labor.[28] With conditions ready-made, Yorke enters and devotes himself to applying the teachings of Leo XIII, which were embodied in his encyclical on the conditions of labor, Rerum Novarum. Cronin's overall interpretation is that Yorke was a social engineer, a reformer.

An interesting letter survives in the Yorke collection in the archives of the University of San Francisco, of interest particularly to those involved in retracing Yorke's career through the works of those who have written about him. Dated October 23, 1940, it was addressed to Father Ralph Hunt, then serving as Yorke's successor as pastor of St. Peter's Church in San Francisco. Hunt had been the youthful, loyal assistant to Yorke in the latter's final years, and after his death unsuccessfully struggled to compile a biography in tribute to his departed chief. Writing from the Catholic University of America, Ph.D. candidate Bernard C. Cronin joyously announced that his dissertation proposal had been accepted by his mentors. Initially hesitant, they accepted the Yorke proposal only after Cronin's "due preparation and some fast talking."[29] Of greater import from the substantive viewpoint is what followed. Cronin, in explaining the details of his proposal, seems to have started with the assumption that the economic scene to be examined was two-sided, finance capital and unskilled labor. Within this framework Cronin intended to place Yorke, who was "advocating and securing the application of the moral principles of Rerum Novarum to industrial relations in San Francisco and elsewhere."[30] Rather than approaching the topic in the form of a problem or question to be tested, Cronin's objective seemed to be narration of Yorke's activities -- activities, which it would appear, had already been interpreted. Yorke, it was assumed, did what he did, because he was moved by deep inner conviction. He wished to reform the community by the application of what was then advanced Papal teaching. In closing, Cronin expressed his gratitude to Yorke's disciple for support and assistance. He was pleased to have his professors accept such a splendid topic -- the labor activities of Father Yorke. "I hope," wrote Cronin, "I can do justice to him in my presentation of his words and works in behalf of labor."[31]

When this undertaking ultimately came to fruition, Yorke did appear as a man who by words and action helped San Francisco toward becoming a union town. Yorke's pro-union behavior was well documented and narrated. To go a step further and generalize to the point of interpreting Yorke as a social reformer devoted to abstract principles seems, however, to generalize beyond the legitimate limits of the hard data which had been developed.

As with the A.P.A. conflict Yorke sides with justice, truth, and fair play, while by implication, his antagonists assume the reverse positions. A basic question, which seems never to have been tested, is: Was Yorke a social reformer or was he, merely, a partisan or militant leader? Confusion seems to have resulted from the fact that in winning his spurs in the A.P.A. conflict and in his later advocacy of union labor, he was clearly in the judgement of history, on the side of justice.

The problem may be one of definition. What is a "reformer?" The history of the struggle of labor to organize and unionize itself in America usually is not viewed as reform history, while pro-labor legislation emanating from state and federal legislative bodies often is so viewed. The educational work of Horace Mann is considered as reform, while the decision to construct an entire system by the Catholic Church seems not to be labeled reform, even by Catholic leadership. A very rough explanation as to why this might be so is that reformers are more easily identified and labeled when they advocate change which has little or no immediate effect on themselves personally. For that reason Wendell Phillips, the new England scion, appears as a reformer while the ex-slave Fredrick Douglass might not, though both men were active abolitionists.

The advocacy of change which is believed to improve the condition of persons other than those with whom the advocate identifies might possibly then be an ingredient within any definition of "reformer." Even here though, problems arise in the transition from the sphere of theory to empiricism. Most who concern themselves with such matters would undoubtedly classify Martin Luther King as a reformer. He worked to alter conditions but in a way so as to be of benefit to those with whom he so closely identified, those who could truly be labeled his own.

Up to this point in the bibliography about Yorke the loosely formulated assumption is that Yorke was a reformer. What he said and did was based on general principles serving the common good and resting on religion, morality, and the general interest. No author seemed concerned that Yorke spoke and acted in behalf of his own, namely Irish-Catholic-labor. A harmony of interests between the good of his own subculture and abstract good was implicitly assumed.

If King can be categorized as a reformer, then why might not Yorke be so labeled? To this writer it seems that there is a minimum requirement basic to determining whether an individual qualifies as a reformer or as a partisan leader: the change or reform being advocated must be equally applicable to the universal population and not restricted to those with shom the advocate most closely identifies. Thus, it is suggested that to demand voting rights for Negroes and deny them to Puerto Ricans, for example, would not qualify one as a reformer.

In approaching San Francisco's labor history with a preconceived conceptual framework which assumed the existence of two separate and antagonistic economic classes, labor and capital, Cronin limited the scope of his study, and almost from the start predetermined his final interpretation. This conceptual framework limited considerations to two dimensions. If instead, the starting point was in the form of a question about the total socio-economic structure of the city, then Yorke could be viewed and assessed against a more sophisticated backdrop, beyond that of the underdog vs the oppressor.

By a simple labor-capital division, important sectors of city life are slighted and ignored. This two-sided division had no place for the urban middle-class, the small shopkeepers, white collar workers, and the professionals who in time came to fear both big business and big unionism.[32] Also, no accurate study of labor in the West can slight the presence of the Chinese. Labor was notoriously anti-Oriental. Since Orientals were not within the fold of union labor and were not Nob Hill capitalists they were not really accounted for in the dichotomized framework. One test of Yorke as a general reformer, as opposed to being merely a partisan leader, could be to determine if the principles he applied to predominantly Irish-Catholic-labor, the subculture of which he was so much a part, were equally applicable in Yorke's mind to other sectors of the city's population, the Chinese and Japanese for example. They too labored and they too were God's children.

After Archbishop Riordan forced Yorke out of the editorship of the local Catholic newspaper,[33] Yorke sojourned in Europe at some length. Upon returning Yorke found himself without a medium whereby he could disseminate the views he felt to be important to the Irish-Catholic community. His words of response to a welcome home reception held in his honor at the Metropolitan Hall in 1899 dripped with self-indulgence and self-justification for his prior behavior.[34] If constant use of the first person singular is an indication, his ego was raw and throbbing. Not only was Yorke cut off from the Chancery and removed from the editorial desk, his Archbishop provided him not even a pulpit upon his return.[35] Languishing without an assignment, like a captain without a barracks, he was taken in by a friend, Father Peter Casey, pastor of St. Peter's. Later Riordan moved him to Oakland and virtual banishment.[36]

Thus cut off from the type of gratification to which he had become accustomed, Yorke started his own weekly, The Leader, in January 1902. Continuing about as long after him as with him, The Leader remains a primary source of information about the Irish-Catholic-labor subculture of San Francisco and on Yorke's activities. It provides unlimited insights into his intellectual life including his convictions concerning another minority sector of the San Francisco population -- the Orientals.

Yorke and Race: A Partisan Leader
    From the first month of The Leader's appearance, Yorke provided his readers a steady diet of articles and editorials dealing with racial questions. Often no difference existed between editorial and news articles, with the two blurring into a single format. For example, progress towards the passing of a Chinese Exclusion Bill in Congress received front page coverage[37] while editorially Yorke came right to the point. To prevent

the working class from sinking to the level of "poor white trash" and to preserve the Pacific Coast as a white man's civilization, Yorke argued that Chinese exclusion was mandatory. He interpreted the Chinese presence in California as a conspiracy of union-busting employers. Yorke urged action in behalf of Oriental exclusion by "everyone who believes that God has reserved California as a home for a free people and a Christian Civilization . . . ."[38] Yorke reasoned the Chinese were such a menace because they made-up a servile class that would not unionize.

The advent of the Russo-Japanese War distracted Yorke from one yellow peril to another. He seemed compelled to announce his sympathies were with Russia.

> Russians are white and the Japs are yellow . . . . The Russians are of Aryan stock, speaking an Aryan language, their thoughts are our thoughts, their ways our ways. The Japs are Mongolians who . . . despise us in their hearts . . . . In the event of an uprising of the yellow millions, California is a frontier province.[39]

Through the years Yorke kept up his sniping at the Japanese. He took note of their alleged moral leprosy,[40] the fact of their attendance at Stanford University,[41] the local stabbing of two "American citizens," one in the groin, by a group of drunken Japs.[42] When the Park Commission decided to make some improvements in the Japanese Tea Garden, after rejecting Yorke's agitation for reduced charges for children's rides at the playground, The Leader observed, "It appears that the Japanese stand in higher favor at the Golden Gate Park than do the little boys and girls of San Francisco."[43] On the famous case of the San Francisco school board's segregation of Oriental children, Yorke fumed at President Theodore Roosevelt's intervention stating, "We have come to a pretty pass if we can't run our own schools."[44]

In fairness to Yorke, however, it should be noted that in his opinion the board policy was in error. The hoped-for objective was for the Japanese children to learn English and become adapted to their new environment. The best way to do this was "by dividing them up among as many schools as possible."[45] He felt on practical grounds that since the total number of school age Japanese was slight, their attendance at a variety of schools would be no inconvenience. He rejected the proposed segregation, then, on the grounds that such a condition would hinder their education -- here interpreting public education to be cultural dunking.

When a San Francisco missionary returned from a tour of the Hawaiian Islands, Yorke published his supporting opinion on race. The inroads made by the Japanese into the economy of the islands were, he felt, "Most hurtful to the progress and prosperity of the country." White men were forced off the islands because they were "unable to compete with the starvation wage living Jap."[46]

These direct and oblique attacks on Orientals may have been no more than periodic column-fillers reflecting a consensus of the news office and editorial office fall-out. Yorke went much further than this, however, in pointed editorials. Warming to the theme, "Race is a Fact," he continued:

It is . . . as certain as any fact can be that the Japanese in California cannot be assimilated as the Irish or English, German, French or Italian are assimilated . . . . The question, therefore, is, are we willing to turn the State of California into a Japanese community?[47]

Yorke's answer, of course, was no. The entire matter was not political or even economic in nature. It was, he felt, "a question of racial destiny." America was half-way between Asia and Europe. The question to Yorke was what was to be America's racial destiny, Asiatic or European?

Here is the Asiatic's opportunity. He can live on . . . much less than the white man -- and therefore is willing to work for less. This state of affairs would be all right if the Asiatics were slaves whose numbers might be regulated and activities directed . . . . There is no way in which one race can live in the midst of another except as master and slave.[48]

When John P. Irish addressed the Commonwealth Club in behalf of the Chinese and Japanese, he and his approach enraged Yorke. Irish approached the problem by comparing the contemporary condition of the Orientals with that of the immigrants from Ireland of days past. If the Orientals would be given at least opportunities equal to Yorke's and his own ethnic group, they too would lift themselves to a status acceptable to Americans generally.

Uncontrolled in his editorial[49] response, Yorke labeled Irish a "sycophant," "renegade," and "wooden ass." He compared the speaker unfavorably to a "razor-backed hog" and suggested that Irish's birth was illegitimate.

Irish-Catholics and Orientals simply were not subject to comparison according to Yorke. Since "half the army that achieved independence was Irish"[50] and Catholics had shed their blood and expended their resources in all American wars, they "were not beggars at the national door, but were children of the household . . . ."[51] Yorke denied that his objection to Asiatic immigration was based on hatred, religion, or even economics. He objected on the grounds that "the American nation can never assimilate the coolie or his race,"[52] and he denied that this was racism.

Further the Oriental was dangerous to America because he was different.

. . . Unrestricted coolie immigration would mean that the problem of the South would be reproduced in the West. There would be two peoples struggling for the possession of the country from the Rockies to the Pacific ocean [sic]. And here we would be dealing not with former slaves or their descendants, naturally docile and of childlike minds, but with the most powerful governments in the world, and with the most astute and unscrupulous statesmen in the service of diplomacy.[53]

Yorke was obsessed by the question of race particularly as it touched the Chinese and Japanese. Undoubtedly this was tied to his commitment to labor unionism in San

Francisco. Since before his arrival in the West, the battle cry of white labor had been, "The Chinese must go,"[54] because another Irishman said so -- Denis Kearney. In 1882 the Irish customs collector at San Francisco did his part by returning Chinese women to Hong Kong labeled arbitrarily as prostitutes.[55] At this same time Chinese laborers were subjected to physical violence at Irish hands, violence from which death was not unknown.[56] This was the local setting when Yorke arrived from Ireland.

Yorke's inflamed views on race, in all likelihood, originated in San Francisco and were based on a tradition of immediate economic competition between Oriental labor -- non-union and low paid -- and his own Irish-Catholic dominated, union-inclined labor subculture. If he entertained views on race during his Irish youth, they were, more likely than not, highly benign, unless, of course, he considered the English a separate race.

As to the Negro in America, Yorke seems to have again absorbed contemporary, local thinking. His views, as reflected in his personal weekly, were those raised to the level of scholarship by U. B. Phillips in American Negro Slavery.[57] For Yorke, the Negro was not a daily personal experience as was the Oriental laborer in San Francisco. Instead he was distant, dociles, and inferior intellectually and culturally.[58] Yorke abominated Negro lynchings.[59] He was repelled by the anti-Negro racism then being disgorged by Thomas Dixon,[60] the onetime classmate of Woodrow Wilson at Johns Hopkins. Dixon had given up the ministry, by this time, in favor of writing plays and novels such as the Clansman, on which the silent film "Birth of a Nation" was later based.[61]

Yorke gave front page coverage to the activities of a newly ordained Negro priest,[62] and he deeply regretted that out of the nine million negroes in the United States, only about 150,000 were Catholics. To overcome what he considered a failure of the Catholic Church, he editorialized for heavy contributions for the special training of more priests for this mission. A special Sunday was set aside for this collection, and he defended it as worthwhile, because when given the opportunity, Negro-Americans did join the church. He viewed their membership as desirable.[63] Still Yorke shared the anti-Negro prejudice of the day. A common figure of speech used by him was, "There is a nigger in the wood-pile . . . ."[64] Anti-Negro jokes were included as space fillers in his weekly, one following a reprint of a sermon by James Cardinal Gibbons.[65] The Ku Klux Klan of Monroe City, Missouri, according to The Leader, consisted of a bunch of the boys and simply reacting to a "crowd of drunken blacks" who had hit Father Thomas Mullen over the head with a whiskey bottle.[66]

Yorke cited Bishop Heslin of Natchez, Mississippi, at great length in The Leader as a Catholic authority on the Negro question. According to the Bisho:

> The great body of blacks are quiet, harmless and tractable; it is
> only a few desperadoes among them that cause the trouble . . . . Lynch-
> ing is savage and barbarous, especially when it assumes the inhuman and
> sickening form of burning at the stake . . . . As it hardly ever . . . happens
> that a Catholic negro is involved in these outrages, I believe the best remedy
> of all would be to bring the negro under the rule and influence of the Catholic

Church.[67]

Having accepted, it would appear, what Wilbur Cash later termed the Southern rape complex,[68] the Bishop concluded, "Let the outrage not be committed and there will be no lynching."[69] He endorsed separation in schools, resorts and transportation and saw no reason for social equality.[70]

In San Francisco Yorke's contact with Negroes was very infrequent, but even then it was unpleasant. He responded to the shooting of an Irish-Catholic stableman by two Negroes by asking, "Are we living in a civilized city or in some African jungle?"[71] The celebrated streetcar strike of 1907, in which the carmen's union took on the grandson of John C. Calhoun and his trolley company,[72] was another occasion when Negroes touched Yorke's sensitive area of interest. His response to this stimulus was at once anti-Semitic, anti-Oriental and anti-Negro. He felt Negro soldiers seen riding "slave driver Calhoun's scab cars" were proper companions for the "jewjap yellow" patrons of the United Railroads.[73]

Since Yorke was a sane and thoughtful man, his words can be used for obtaining insights into his mind. He opposed Orientals primarily because as laborers they worked for less than what a white man preferred. He identified with union labor since so many within his own subculture were within its ranks. Implicit within his statements is a highly interesting system of categories. The Chinese were excluded from his definition of the working-class, with San Francisco's population consisting of capitalists, workers, and Chinese. In mutually exclusive and conflicting categories, he placed Japanese on the one hand, and boys and girls of San Francisco on the other. Being quite the logician used to syllogistic reasoning,[74] Yorke undoubtedly could come up with a rational explanation for all this. Nonetheless, he wrote, consciously or not, on the implied assumption that Orientals were of a category unto themselves, if not a separate creation. Since unionization in San Francisco was exclusive rather than inclusive from the start,[75] Yorke was correct in excluding Orientals from the category of union labor, but not in excluding them from the labor force.

At the start of the decade in which Yorke worried most about the impending uprising of the yellow millions, San Francisco's Oriental population totaled 15,735[76] or 4.3 percent of the total city population -- a net drop of 40 percent in the Oriental sector since 1890. Here there is one basic difference between local anti-Catholicism of the 1870's and Yorke's fear of the yellow menace of the 1900's. The paranoids of the seventies seemed to agree with the editor of Thistleton's Illustrated . . . in that if ignorant papists revolted, they would be whipped by the enlightened majority.[77] Yorke shared no such confidence decades later.

By portraying Asiatics as dangerous to American institutions, he hurled the very same charges which the American Protective Association threw at the Catholic Church the decade before. The only distinction drawn by Yorke was that such charges were untrue for the Catholic Irish, but true for Orientals. His speculation on Oriental slavery, with his statement that within such a society, population control could be maintained, only demonstrates in the most graphic form his total exclusion of this group from the principles of Rerum Novarum. If Yorke was a social reformer, he was a rather selective one. He championed the cause of his own people with energy, talent and persistence at a time when they were located in a marginal position on the socio-economic spectrum. His advocacy was not always aimed at those in a more advanced position. By advancing the cause of Irish-Catholic labor, partially at the expense of the even less advantaged, "partisan leader" seems much more appropriate than "reformer" as Yorke's title.

Was Yorke an Intellectual?

Among those who have deeply considered the American experience of the Irish, at least two have posited generalizations that the behavior of Yorke, here considered, appears to substantiate. The Irish in America have not been noted as ideologists, as true believers who know what is best through philosophical means and then attempt to force their truth on the body politic. Instead that have been recognized as facilitators of other men's ideas.[78] In other words, they acquire their sense of direction from their environment. This is Oscar Handlin's interpretation of Al Smith, in that once out of politics and isolated, he turned from a liberal to a reactionary.[79] This interpretation also runs through the two volume biography of Cardinal Gibbons by John Tracy Ellis. Gibbons was not an original thinker. He sought other men's ideas and tried to create a consensus, one he then would prod in a progressive direction. Unlike Smith, he never was defeated in an election and never became a reactionary.

As has been amply proven by Gaffey, Yorke was not an organization man. That he did not seek consensus is also amply clear. He gloried in conflict. His predisposition toward the Chinese really was no different than his predisposition toward the Negro. Yet in San Francisco, he seems to have developed racists views of a volatile nature regarding the former -- an identified, present threat -- and rather benign attitudes in regard to the latter, which was distant. This fact of his views being so strongly influenced, if not determined, by very local and peculiar phenomena, as opposed to a more liberated and detached view drawn from sources beyond the physical and economic realities of day to day subcultural life, might tend to suggest that not only was Yorke not a reformer, but that probably he was not even an intellectual. In order to test such a hypothesis, more data seem necessary which touch on more relevant areas of Yorke's interests.

Considerable evidence exists which demonstrates that Father Yorke was intelligent and learned. Throughout his press war with the A.P.A., he was forced to do research and write on a wide variety of topics, ranging through philosophy, sociology and history. For example, he explained such diverse phenomena as the number of Catholic convicts in San Quentin and the views of Robert Bellarmine on the burning of heretics.[80] His surviving early papers reveal lecture texts and outlines meticulously prepared both in English and Gaelic.[81] His readings on the history of the United States took him through the writings of Henry Adams and French and Latin American authors. His notes are in English, French and Spanish depending on the language of the text.[82] He kept up on book reviews and maintained an account with the Macmillan Company and London book dealers. The latter were commissioned to search for rare books in which

Yorke was interested.[83]

Among his collected and published works are twenty-one volumes, of which four deal largely with political and educational topics of his day. The remainder are school books for children, at various elementary grade levels, in which he dealt with the Catholic religion. Merely a sample of these items reveals that learning, intelligence and thought were required for their compilation. His 1905 Lenten lectures at St. Anthony's Parish in Oakland, California, were covered in the daily press at great length and quite favorably. In these presentations he treated the history of the Catholic Church. They were learned and reflected his reading and contemplation.[84]

Yorke held conventional views on the nature of man. According to him, man was a duality composed of body and soul, matter and mind. Man's matter, his body, belongs to the animal world with all its animal wants and becomes an "ugly brute" when these wants are neglected. Mind was considered to be of a higher order, its task being to restrain and guide the animal through reason. Basic to the nature of man is unending conflict between this higher and lower self. Man, therefore, is a child of light and darkness. "His roots are in the earth; but his head is in the heavens."[85]

In 1900 Yorke extended this basic doctrine a step further in a sermon entitled "The Secular Conflict." The warfare he saw raging between body and soul is not confined to the individual, but exists in society with the things of the world warring on the Kingdom of God. This was Yorke's "secular conflict." The sides were "dissimilar," and their principles were "diametrically opposed." Yorke placed on the side of evil all the things in which the world rejoices. In this category he included wealth, position, power, and pleasure, and also wit and intellect. Opposed to this catalogue were ". . . the poor in spirit, the meek, the merciful, the mourners, the persecuted, the clean of heart." In juxtaposition to Christ's beatitudes from His Sermon on the Mount, Yorke placed intellect and wisdom. In thinly veiled sarcasm, he concluded that, "Against the wisdom of the world stands the foolishness of the Gospel."[86]

Yorke on Universities

Throughout his life Yorke wrote and said many things, not all of which are entirely compatible. But in his pulpit and in his published works, this intelligent priest told his working class subculture that seeking God and seeking the intellectual life on earth were all but incompatible activities.[87] Never a respecter of institutions, Yorke, after the founding of his Leader, repeatedly held up to criticism and scorn the institutional manifestations of the intellectual life. While he periodically claimed to be only criticizing the particular administration of respective universities , his broadsides were applied with such a wide brush that only the most discriminating observer would recognize such behavior as anything other than a general indictment.

The national symbols from which Yorke seemed alienated were the East, Harvard, and the other Ivy League universities.[88] Locally his discontent focused on Stanford University and the University of California. In addition to charging maladministration, he maintained that they were hostile to Catholicism and discriminated against

Catholics. His criticisms of university life, however, were not restricted to secular institutions, but in many ways, Yorke was most vicious with his own alma mater, the Catholic University of America, its administration and some faculty.

Yorke had been associated with the Catholic University from its opening day as one of its charter students in 1889. His Archbishop had been a supporter of the institution at a time when the Catholic hierarchy was far less than unanimous concerning its creation and development.[89] As a young priest sent there for graduate studies in theology, he was, undoubtedly, aware of the tenuous nature of the institution's existence and hope for survival. As a graduate student on this campus, Yorke was unhappy and persevered only after direct pressure applied by his Archbishop, who used the word "sorehead" to describe Yorke's behavior.[90] The fact of his being invited later to stay on as a faculty member, seems to have had no endearing effect on Yorke.

His first public challenge to the University appeared during the very first month of his paper's publication. He disagreed with action taken by the Academic Senate, recommended by the Rector and approved by the Trustees, concerning a personnel matter. The matter was complicated by Irish nationalism and the charge of financial mismanagement.

The Ancient Order of Hibernians, a national organization in the United States devoted to Irish nationalism and cultural preservation, had contributed $50,000 to the struggling young University for the purpose of advancing the Gaelic language. The University responded by obtaining a professor of Gaelic from Maynooth College in Ireland, Father Richard Henebry, for the teaching assignment. He was given a three year contract without tenure, continuance and tenure to be determined at the expiration of the contract.[91] Henebry wished to begin his appointment immediately, but the University, very much to its credit considering its meager resources, sent him to Germany for two years where he earned his Ph.D. Joining the Catholic University faculty in the fall of 1898, he quickly entered Irish-American political activities as an alien in the United States and was elected President of the Gaelic League of America.[92] Yorke served as President of the California chapter. When the matter of his reappointment was brought before the Academic Senate in the spring of 1901, the faculty voted that Henebry not be reappointed. The Board of Trustees concurred in the faculty decision.[93]

Henebry refused to accept this action as the accomplished fact, even when receiving the word from Cardinal Gibbons himself, and he drew full support from Father Yorke. Yorke maintained that Henebry was cashiered because of his political activities, while the university -- trustees, administration, and faculty -- maintained nonperformance of duty. The fact was that Henebry had been ill during his three year appointment. He once traveled to London to consult with a physician who in turn recommended rest in the American Southwest, a maneuver which, undoubtedly, appeared to be a long way from the doctor's office to the drugstore from the vantage point of Washington, D.C.[94]

Yorke roundly attacked the University generally as the preserve of "Anglo-Irish American Churchmen,"[95] claiming that "They have driven out Dr. Henebry because he is an Irishman."[96] The first Catholic University academician to be muckraked by Yorke was its Rector, Bishop Thomas J. Conaty. He had been appointed by Rome on the recommendation of the Trustees when the fortunes of the University were ebbing low. His liberal predecessor had been deposed by the Pope[97] at a time when the American Catholic community seems simply to have lacked well qualified educators of stature from which to draw a prestigous successor.[98] Irish born, the oldest of eight, Conaty was brought to America at the age of three. At sixteen he entered the seminary, and in this environment his formal education was completed.[99] Prior to his appointment as Rector, his limited reputation rested on his activities for temperance, Irish nationalism, and running a Catholic summer school. During the term of his appointment, he worked to the best of his ability to keep the University afloat and prevent it from dissolving from internal factionalism. He was unable to do this successfully, and when his term expired, it was simply a question of providing him with a place of dignity. Cardinal Gibbons, the Chancellor of the University was unwilling to abandon and forget him.[100]

At the very time when Yorke's own Archbishop was working with Gibbons to secure a place in California for Conaty,[101] Yorke publicly branded him as incompetent.

Dr. Conaty is a D.D., to be sure, but his one claim to learning is a little book which he published for Sunday school and which is so raw that it was received with a universal howl of derision. It might be creditable as the performance of a seventh-grade schoolboy, but, as the work of a University Rector -- Ye Gods!

Indeed, so limited are the good Doctor's attainments that when he was proposed first a distinguished Archbishop and Regent of the University declared that it would smother the University in New England with laughter.[102]

Bitter sarcasm was the tone adopted by Yorke concerning the University faculty. He admitted that the school was strong in the language department since "the professors there are mostly all double-tongued."[103] An exception to this rule, however, was Professor Maurice F. Egan of the English department who, according to Yorke:

. . . is good enough to look over copybooks, correct exercises and do the menial work of English Literature, but he knows absolutely nothing about its scientific aspects and he is too busy editing bunkum books for the Catholic trade to learn.[104]

Yorke also challenged the academic qualifications of Professor Thomas J. Shahan. Yorke admitted Shahan lectured and published, but both, in his judgement, while nicely worded were devoid of thought and any evidence of research. And more than that, his articles did not appear in journals of eminence. Yorke publicly held up to scorn for his working-class readers the quality of a professor's publications and the prestige of the journals in which they appeared. Yorke switched criteria, however, for the comparative advantage of his fellow ethnic activist. Henebry was a professor of quality because of what he would accomplish in the unknown future. Yorke disregarded Henebry's lack of scholarly accomplishments to date, and claimed, "Dr. Henebry has the entre [sic] to the most exclusive magazines in Europe . . . ."[105]

Judged by any standard, intelligence, knowledge, work done, manliness, Dr. Henebry is head and shoulders above his chief opponents, Drs. Conaty and Shahan.[106]

Before Yorke moved on to newer issues, he leveled one parting blast at the Catholic University's scarcity of students, a condition hardly assisted by the quality of his journalism.

The Catholic University is booming, or expected to boom this coming year. Each professor is pretty certain to have as many as three students in his class . . . . Besides, Dr. Shahan and Dr. Egan are said to be contemplating taking up Keltic under young Mr. Dunne -- when he has become educated.[107]

Dunne, according to Yorke was "a native born, a full-blooded Anglo-Saxon-Irish-American, a graduate of Harvard, don't you-know, who after a little study in Yerrup, will-aw-be a much better and satisfactory person than a mere Irishman aw! don't-you-know."[108] Throughout the controversy Yorke held Harvard up to derision, as if that institution symbolized hypocrisy and fraud. When a Harvard professor of Gaelic -- probably the only one in America -- delivered lectures on his discipline at the Catholic University, after Henebry had been let go, Yorke linked him to his institution and denounced him for having "acted the part of the scab" for doing "what a decent longshoreman would shrink from in horror."[109]

Professors, Harvard, and the intellectual life generally did not benefit from this analogy in the minds of Yorke's unionized followers. In effect, Yorke told Irish-Catholic labor, in the crudest of terms, not to aspire to sending their sons to Harvard. Harvard was for snobs. Neither should they aspire to the Catholic University. There the faculty was incompetent and the institution, itself, verged on dissolution.

Each of Yorke's several sorties against academia were highly charged with personal invective. In the Catholic University case, he rallied to the support of a fellow activist against individuals he arbitrarily labeled Anglo-Irish. His conflict with Stanford University, devoid of the intra-Irish squabbles, was also supercharged with personal animosity. Yorke's public statements were highly volatile due to the fact he seldom separated the issues from their advocates, and when he did, he attacked the advocates. Yorke's problem with Stanford centered on the new Stanford chapel and its proposed brand of relition, nondenominationalism. Yorke did address himself to the question of the common denominator approach to religion, but only in the most flippant of ways. He asked, for example:

Will the new religion of Stanford insist on one wife with the Episcopalians, or four with the Mohammedans, or as many as a graduate can support with the Mormons? Will it echo the Jewish command, "Honor thy father and thy mother," or will it adopt the interesting practise of certain . . . Christians of Central Africa who considerately boil and eat their aged relatives?[110]

But even here Yorke did not remain above the level of personal insinuation, stating, "of sourse genetic reasons will forbid a religion for Stanford University to insist on the commandment, 'Thou shalt not steal.'"[111] The insinuation, of course, questioned the means whereby the Stanfords had obtained their wealth in railroad construction.

The prime concern of Yorke with Stanford was its chapel. He viewed nonsectarianism as simply another sect and more damnable because of its pretense and hypocrisy. The dedication of the chapel marked the point for Yorke from which Stanford University was to be regarded as a "frank foe" of the Catholic Church. The new University was installing "its own religion as it installs its own kitchen and its own sewers."[112]

As every, Yorke's strongest punches were body blows to individuals. The new minister installed at Stanford, Reverend Heber Newton, was depicted as an Eastern "bigot" and Rome baiter,[113] who in his dedication sermon ran on with ". . . the conventional Protestant soft soap for Romanists -- claptrap about cathedrals and twaddle about art . . . ."[114]

> . . . the new religion of Stanford will consist mainly of an aching void
> . . . . Rev. Heber Newton will be able to shovel words therein a plenty
> for in that precisely does his dishonesty consist. He steals the clothes
> of Christianity to cover his putrid sores . . . . Sham Christian, sham
> Episcopalian, he was cut out to be the apostle of a sham religion in a
> University that from the bottom of its foundations to the top of its spire is
> one great symphony of sham.[115]

Before he felt he had finished with Stanford, Yorke painted Mrs. Leland Stanford as a pathetic little woman who talked about God as a loving father, while the well paid anti-God professors sneered at the Catholic Church in her classrooms.[116] President David Starr Jordan was simply an educated fool who had substituted the "spinal cord for the Almighty."[117] And in the end he predicted the ultimate failure of Stanford as an institution of higher learning because of its position on religion.[118] He noted its continuing diptheria and typhoid problems and recommended that the State Board of Health keep a close watch on Stanford.[119]

The subject of higher education for members of his own San Francisco subculture is one that deeply concerned Yorke. As ever, he held strong views. He felt the Irish were missing the boat due to their own lack of appreciation of the value of education. Probably to the amazement of his working class readers, he occasionally advocated a college education for their children almost as forcefully as he muckraked professors, presidents and universities. He advised Irish parents to follow the example set by the Jews, not to let the lads drop-out for an early job. This was poor economy in the long run.[120] To get ahead in the world higher education was vital, and the best place to obtain such an education was under the auspices of the Catholic Church.

> . . . a Catholic school is the safest place for a Catholic child and parents
> should pause before they deprive their children of the advantages of a Christian education when they can have it at a very little sacrifice.[121]

For those young people within Yorke's Irish-Catholic-labor community who sought after an intellectual life, either within the Catholic schools or beyond, the experience could have been nothing short of traumatic. For their parents it could have brought only agony. From Yorke's encounter with Stanford non-sectarianism, it would appear he felt, at least within the sphere of religion, that all truth was known. That Yorke possessed it went without saying. All that remained was the application of dogma to specific circumstances. To deal with knowledge as expanding and tentative would, he felt, have a disastrous effect on the student mind. Without dogma the student might become confused. [122] Yorke was quite clear on the assigned role of all members of the laity within the Catholic Church. "By divine appointment the clergy rules . . . . There is a Church teaching and a Church taught. To the Church taught the laity belongs. "[123] Yorke considered this a guiding principle to be applied to Catholics who were college graduates. For a man to qualify as a Catholic leader, Yorke maintained he must gain his distinction in the field of church activity, and as he cast the roles, slight opportunity, indeed, existed for the layman. [124] To obtain recognition in scholarly or other intellectual pursuits carried no weight with Yorke.

In the midst of Yorke's assaults on Stanford, eleven Catholic students at that institution objected to his treatment of their University. He retorted with sarcasm, ridicule, and belittlement, pushed on by a pulsating ego. First, they were young, next they were students, and as such were subject to the same clerical directives as the "hodcarrier." As university students they were immature with a "lopsided education" full of pride and vanity. To their request for fair play, Yorke responded with the common working-class stereotype of collegiate life -- thievery, drunkenness, gambling and libertine behavior. He alleged that by selecting pagan Stanford, they had chosen Caesar rather than God. They, the "heirs of nineteen centuries of Christian culture and teaching," were hanging their heads "before the descendants of the Anglo-Saxon Swineherds. "[125] They had denied their heritage at Stanford in order to obtain material advantages and to cultivate their minds.

> When the incense is in their hand for Diana's altar, when the knee is bent to Caesar why recall them to the presence of their God and the image of the Crucified. Let us alone is their cry. We are too loyal to our Alma Mater . . . . We do not want to choose; but if you will compel us to choose, we must remember our chivalry and the bread we have eaten. So God help us, the choice is made, and the sons of the martyrs pass through the fire to Maloch. [126]

The example held up by Yorke for the young students in his own parish school to imitate was not the example of those young collegiates who were trying to look beyond the contemporary bounds of their own subculture, but rather the intellectual example of the Knights of Columbus. These men didn't waste their time, Yorke maintained, reading novels, but stocked their houses with good Catholic books, magazines and papers. "They know about our Holy Father the Pope . . . , his trials and his troubles, about Catholics in other lands." These men kept up as they should "with the best Catholic thought of the day. "[127] This was a level of intellectual activities and an expanse of cultural vistas toward which Catholics might safely aspire.

Yorke reflected the view that attendance at a state university was an "evil," and a job of the Catholic Church was to minimize this evil for the "unfortunate Catholic students" who were caught in this set of circumstances.[128] Yorke let few chances slip when he could portray state or private schools in a poor light. And always his medium of presentation remained his personal paper. It entered working class homes which in time would be able to send children out for more schooling. Over and over, these parents were told Harvard symbolized the Hydra.

In the first place, Harvard and other comparable institutions were only a sham. To Yorke they were the "Alma Maters of the 'rah, rah' contingent" and respected only by the "uninformed."[129] Yorke responded to an anonymous campaign slur against an Irish candidate for the presidency of the Harvard Democratic Club by noting anti-Catholicism was strong at Harvard as at all similar colleges. He went on to suggest that Catholics who enrolled themselves in such institutions opened themselves up for insults, and rather than patronizing "the Harvard snobs," they should be more loyal to their own Catholic colleges.[130] Besides, only "Catholic snobs" sent their children to secular universities. "These flunkey Catholics generally think more of the exactions of society than they do of the commandments of the Church . . . ."[131]

Judging from what could be read in The Leader, a parent threw the temporal and spiritual well-being of his child to the wind when he sent him off to a prestigous university. At Harvard, they were informed, ninety percent of the freshmen and ninety-five percent of the seniors drank. Thirty-five percent drank heavily and sixty-five percent went wild on wine and bad women. Drinking and gambling were worse at Columbia, followed by Harvard, Princeton and Cornell. On one occasion at Princeton, Yorke informed his Irish-Catholic readers that over three hundred students were dead drunk. Due to its favored geographic position, Columbia led in the category of debauchery. Twelve-thousand graduates of "the big secular universities" were held to be inhabitants of slums, jails, and sanitariums as a result of fast living.

The data on which this muckraking of the institutional embodiment of the intellectual life was based came from a trade journal, The Valve World, in which an allegedly wealthy iron man had revealed his personal "research" findings. In such The Leader had a corroborating witness.[132]

The Leader and the Intellect

Considerable confusion existed in the Catholic community of San Francisco as to the official status of The Leader. The bankrupt relationship between Yorke and Archbishop Riordan was not common knowledge, for Riordan had never repudiated Yorke publicly. In 1909, Riordan admitted to Archbishop Diomede Falconio, the apostolic delegate, that The Leader, in the minds of local Catholics, was considered of equal authority with the official church paper, The Monitor.[133] And under Yorke, it spoke with greater vigor and spice. Riordan had forbade his clergy from participating in political activity, but Yorke continued to wallow in it. Occasionally Yorke made gestures toward compiance, but somehow the end result desired by his Archbishop seemed always to be frustrated.[134]

Yorke founded The Leader in 1902 while deeply involved in the advocacy of union labor. The paper was devoted to this cause through the years, but with the emphasis gradually favoring Irish nationalism and related subcultural interests. A highly militant weekly, its masthead announced, "You need a paper to champion your cause, and one that is ever on the side of right." The editorial policy was persistently combative and seemed always to portray a comfortable harmony of interest -- what was good for Irish-Catholic-labor, as determined by Yorke, was also on the side of abstract right.

The paper seems also to have performed an important function for Yorke. He was an intelligent and aggressive activist whose ego would not allow him to preside over the destinies of his parish alone. Since he was denied access to the formal apparatus of church administration, The Leader became a new outlet for his views which he correctly believed people wanted to hear. Through The Leader editorials and news columns, he was able to justify his behavior, compliment himself, and take pot shots at his opponents or former friends.[135] In its statement of editorial policy, The Leader claimed to be nonpartisan with the editor's function being the relation of daily events to "correct principles." The bulk of the subscribers were Irish-Catholics, and the paper included subjects about which they were interested.[136] The paper appeared to be in good financial condition through Yorke's life and probably was. Subscriptions were a dollar a year, at first, and advertisements were significant. In 1903, the size was expanded to seven columns per page, with an average of eight pages per issue. The Call and Hearst newspapers advertised themselves in The Leader, and at election time, candidates of all parties did the same.[137]

One theme which permeated The Leader, often latent, sometimes blatant, was anti-intellectualism. As has been noted already, the institutionalized adjuncts to the intellectual life were not generally advanced by Yorke's pen. Through 1907, he featured a Mr. Dooley type character called Professor Schnortz, whom he engaged in first person conversation concerning current issues.[138] The professor was presented as somewhat of an educated snob who did no real work to justify his existence. The setting was Yorke's editorial office rather than Dooley's pub. The professor would stop in weekly, display his ornamental education and regret the realistic, hard working editor's lack of the same.[139] Whenever Schnortz ran out of something to say, the editor would feed him a straight line. Through what was almost a monologue, the professor indicated he made his living at literature, enjoyed novel reading, and occasionally attended church in order not to lose contact with the less enlightened, and to sop up local color.[140] All were clearly designed attributes which would orient Irish-Catholic-labor in the reverse direction. The editor and the professor did agree on one issue, however, the advisability of college students not joining Greek societies. Before responding to a supposed letter to the editor, the editor consulted with the professor who was more knowledgeable in such things. A distressed mother, the writer, wanted only the best advantages for her daughter. Her husband, a good "Union man," opposed sororities because "them Greeks are no good . . . cheap labor guys who can't talk so as to be understood, and . . . he won't have no black hand in his family . . . ."[141] Beyond this they agreed on nothing.

In discussing the race question as related to the Japanese, no such harmony existed between editor and professor. The editor's lines followed the standard anti-Japanese, patriotic thrust of the day. The professor, not required to earn a living through honest labor in competition with the Japanese, took a detached view. He seemed pleased that the end result in California would be Japanese economic dominance, accompanied by a high degree of miscegenation and significant interracial adultery, besides. In light of conventional Irish-Catholic morality and union labor views on the Japanese as a social and economic threat, the professor uttered the nasty lines which baited subscribers. As he turned to leave the editor's office, Schnortz recommended that to stay in business under the new Japanese order, a Japanese section ought to be started in the paper.[142]

To define what is meant by an "intellectual" is indeed difficult. Yorke never defined the term, but simply worked through symbols like the professor. Little agreement exists over the question, who is an intellectual. Yorke, on occasion, treated the institutional accompaniments to the intellectual life in a shameful manner. Harvard and Ivy League were often held up to scorn. The Catholic University of America and Stanford were the objects of his most persistent attacks. The professor in the abstract was satirized, while individual academic types were muckraked before Yorke's working-class patrons. In the case of Catholic students at Stanford, he arranged the circumstances so that to remain at the University was to reject their religion, race, and family circumstances. If their attempts were toward broadening their world view beyond the confines of their subculture, Yorke's behavior and prestige did not encourage them in that adventure.

In each of these cases Yorke dealt not with that elusive concept, the intellectual life, but rather its institutional manifestations. His effect on the minds of his working-class followers was undoubtedly to discredit the intellectual life in general, along with its specific trappings. While significant, this, in itself, is insufficient justification, however, for clearly labeling Yorke an anti-intellectual. Only in the Schnortz case did he satirize the professor in the abstract. That he attacked individual universities and professors is correct. But since the degree to which these particular cases accurately reflected the intellectual life is not readily measurable, more direct analysis of Yorke's mind seems needed.

Yorke's Use of His Intellect

Yorke's personal activity of an intellectual nature seemed always to be sparked by outside forces presenting him with a problem. He would analyze the problem, mobilize his resources and bring forth a solution. In this manner he might be compared to Benjamin Franklin. For example, in colonial Pennsylvania more people died in the winter than summer. Population growth was desirable, and so Franklin invented a more efficient stove. When riding in the country he liked to read and enjoy the view alternately, but disliked changing glasses, therefore, bifocals. For Franklin to qualify as an intellectual, his activities in science must be evaluated, otherwise, he remains a clever lowbrow. Only in science did he lose himself in the pursuit of knowledge. He examined a phenomenon simply because it interested him.[143] For awhile he even felt guilty because his time was spent at something which might have no practical result.

But then this bothered him less when he felt, so what.

In Yorke's case the A.P.A. presented an external problem against which he reacted. The <u>Baltimore Catechism</u> and the Sisters' inability to teach it, was another problem presented from beyond the confines of his own mind, a problem which provoked a Yorke solution -- text books.

Unlike Franklin and science, no sector of Yorke's secular life seems to have been motivated from within. What brought forth his best efforts were pressure and conflict from outside sources -- antagonists to be put in their place, practical problems to be solved.

As has been seen,[144] he saw man and society in conflict within themselves. On one side were Christian beatitudes. On the other was the intellect. And the two were incompatible. Yorke was a highly intelligent person, but he seems to have used the intellectual life as simply another weapon in his arsenal with which to club his personal, political, religious, and economic adversaries. A close look at one of his intellectual exercises illustrates the point.

On April 23, 1896, Yorke delivered a lecture in his anti-A.P.A. series. Intrinsic evidence indicates it was well researched and well prepared. Applause noted on the transcript copy indicates it was very well received by a sympathetic audience.[145] The evening's topic was a historical analysis of the institution of slavery in the New World. The emphasis was placed on the role of the Catholic Church as implemented by Spain and Portugal and compared with that of Protestant England. Some of his views in comparing slavery in Latin America with what existed in the English colonies and later in the United States foreshadowed the work of Stanley Elkins.[146] Unlike Elkins, however, Yorke sought no new insights. He sought to use an academic discipline to serve his immediate, practical purpose. In the process, the integrity of history was brutalized for factional religious advantage. In the case of England, the seeds of slavery and all its evils were "sown by that pious Queen Elizabeth," while in the Spanish case the evils were "what we might expect from rough men cast away from civilization."[147] In the Protestant case, slavery was masterminded by the careful plan of a supposedly religious and enlightened sovereign. In the Catholic case, the cause stemmed from individual convicts who had been part of the Spanish crews.

Yorke cited the Portuguese slave traders as motivated by economic profit. He also noted the English abolition movement. Both, however, were interpreted as deviant patterns of behavior running counter to the norms.[148] The critical difference between English Protestant behavior in North America and Catholic behavior in Latin America, Yorke maintained, was the treatment of the Indian. In North America he was destroyed, while to the south " . . . the Indian is master in his father's halls."[149] The reason for Indians being spared from slavery in Latin America was attributed to Las Casas and other priests fighting in their behalf. Yorke concluded:

> . . . in a Catholic country governed by Catholic ideas, it became impossible
> for slavery to grow. In fifty years from the discovery of America, this

[Indian] slavery . . . was cut down. It was cut down . . . because monks and priests and the Pope were ready to stand between the down-trodden Indian and his haughty master, and were able to curb that haughty master by the power of religious principles . . . .[150]

Criticism of Yorke here is complicated by the fact there has been an avalanche of data and interpretations on this problem since he wrote and spoke the above. Admittedly, Yorke overstated the position of the Latin American Indian. His major thrust, however, that Catholic institutions moderated slavery in Latin America, has been accepted widely, but the thesis is more often applied to the Negro rather than the Indian.[151] Also, Yorke either did not know or else omitted the fact that Las Casas advocated, at least for awhile, Negro slavery in order to prevent liquidation of his Indians under the system.[152] Yorke must have known of the existence of Negro slavery in Latin America, for in Catholic Brazil, it persevered until 1888, but it was the Indians who received his attention.

By foreshadowing the interpretation of Tannenbaum and Elkins, Yorke demonstrated that ideas of a partisan should not be rejected because he is a partisan. But his selectivity and biased interpretations, particularly as to attributed motivation, seem not in harmony with the goals toward which intellectuals should strive. Yorke, in this case, selected a problem and supporting data which displayed his religion in more favorable terms than his opponent's. In the process, history as a discipline did not profit, and while his audience thoroughly enjoyed the evening, one wonders if their long range intellectual well-being was really served.

Yes, Yorke was intelligent. To label him an intellectual is risky, to classify him with Newman is absurd.

[1] Statement made by Monseigneur Harold Collins to the author, San Francisco, June 4, 1969; James P. Gaffey, The Life of Patrick William Riordan: Second Archbishop of San Francisco, 1841-1914 (Ph.D. dissertation, Catholic University of America, 1965), p. 148.

[2] Yorke diary excerpt, August 14, 1924, Yorke Collection, Archives of the University of San Francisco, hereafter cited AUSF.

[3] Collins interview, June 4, 1969.

[4] John Tracy Ellis, American Catholicism (Chicago: University of Chicago, 1956), p. 49.

[5] Collins interview, June 4, 1969.

[6] Gaffey, op.cit., p.148.

[7] Ibid., pp.378-81.

[8] Ray Allen Billington, The Protestant Crusade, 1800-1860 (Chicago: Quadrangle, 1964); John Higham, Strangers in the Land: Patterns of American Nativism, 1860-1925 (New York: Atheneum, 1965).

[9] Twelfth Census of the United States, 1900, United States Census Office, (Washington: 1901), I, 738-9.

[10] See chart page 16.

[11] Joseph S. Brusher, S.J., "Peter C. Yorke and the A.P.A. in San Francisco," The Catholic Historical Review, XXXVII (July, 1951), p.134.

[12] John Tracy Ellis, Documents of American Catholic History (Milwaukee: Bruce, 1962), pp. 480-1.

[13] Brusher, "Peter C. Yorke and the A.P.A. . . . .," p.135.

[14] Included within each group by way of definition are those born in these foreign countries and those with at least one parent born in these foreign countries.

[15] Gaffey, op.cit., p.160.

[16] For more on this "marginal man" see Arthur Mann's Introduction to William L. Riordon, ed., Plunkitt of Tammany Hall (New York: E. P. Dutton, 1963), xv.

[17] George E. Mowry, <u>The California Progressives</u> (Chicago: Quadrangle, 1963), pp. 7-8.

[18] Gaffey cited Priscilla F. Kunth, <u>Nativism in California</u> (M.A. thesis, University of California, Berkeley, 1947), p. 157-73.

[19] Gaffey, <u>op. cit.</u>, pp. 362-3.

[20] <u>Religious Bodies, 1906</u>, U.S. Department of Commerce and Labor, Bureau of the Census, pt. I, (Washington: 1910), pp. 299-300.

[21] "Souvenir St. Peter's Church Picnic and Reunion, June 21st, 1900," Yorke Collection, AUSF.

[22] David J. Herlihy, "Battle Against Bigotry: Father Peter C. Yorke and the American Protective Association in San Francisco, 1893-1897," <u>Records of the American Catholic Historical Society of Philadelphia</u>, IXII (June, 1951), p. 98.

[23] Ibid., p. 99.

[24] See also Walton Bean, <u>Boss Ruef's San Francisco: The Story of the Union Labor Party, Big Business, and the Graft Prosecution</u> (Berkeley: University of California, 1952) p. 220; Michael Rogin, "Progressivism and the California Electorate," <u>The Journal of American History</u>, LV (Sept., 1968), pp. 299-305.

[25] Gaffey, op. cit., p. 400.

[26] Brusher, "Peter C. Yorke and the A.P.A. . . . ," pp. 149-50.

[27] Lee Benson, <u>The Concept of Jacksonian Democracy</u>, (New York: Atheneum, 1964), pp. 281-7; Raymond E. Wolfinger, "The Development and Persistence of Ethnic Voting," <u>The American Political Science Review</u>, LIX (Dec., 1965), pp. 896-908.

[28] Bernard C. Cronin, <u>Father Yorke and the Labor Movement in San Francisco, 1900-1910</u> (Washington D.C.: Catholic University of America, 1943), p. 14.

[29] Bernard C. Cronin to Father Hunt, Washington, D.C., October 23, 1940, Yorke Collection, AUSF.

[30] <u>Loc. cit.</u>

[31] <u>Loc cit.</u>

[32] Mowry, op. cit., pp. 92-3; Richard Hofstadter, <u>The Age of Reform</u> (New York: Vintage, 1960), pp. 148-64.

[33] Gaffey, op.cit., p.409.

[34] "Response of Rev. Father P. C. Yorke, Metropolitan Hall, San Francisco, November 13, 1899," Yorke Collection, AUSF.

[35] Gaffey, op.cit., p.415.

[36] To be moved out of San Francisco was desired by no priest at this time. For Irishmen it carried the added humiliation of a provential return address to be noted by friends and colleagues in Ireland. Collins interview, June 4, 1969.

[37] The Leader, Jan. 25, 1902.

[38] Ibid., Feb. 15, 1902.

[39] Ibid., Feb. 29, 1904.

[40] Ibid., July 2, 1904.

[41] Ibid., Jan. 26, 1907.

[42] Ibid., June 1, 1907.

[43] Ibid., April 10, 1909.

[44] Ibid., Dec. 8, 1906.

[45] Ibid., Feb. 9, 1907.

[46] Ibid., Feb. 2, 1907.

[47] Ibid., Dec. 8, 1906.

[48] Ibid., Sept. 14, 1907. For more on Mongolian hegemony in California laced with anti-Semitism see The Leader, Feb. 15, 1908.

[49] Ibid., Sept. 25, 1909.

[50] Loc. cit.

[51] Loc. cit.

[52] Loc. cit.

[53] Loc cit.,

[54] John W. Caughey, California (2nd ed.: Englewood Cliffs: Prentice-Hall, 1960), p. 388.

[55] John S. Mosby to E. L. Sullivan, Hong Kong, May 9, 1882, copy included in Consular Dispatches, Hong Kong, 1882-1884, Department of State, General Records, vol. 14, (Record Group 59), National Archives, Washington, D.C.

[56] Tsu Shau Pang to Frederick J. Frelinghuysen, Washington, D.C., May 29, 1882, Notes from the Chinese Legation, 1868-1906, Department of State, General Records, (Record Group 59), National Archives, Washington, D.C.

[57] Ulrich B. Phillips, American Negro Slavery (New York: Appleton, 1918).

[58] Yorke lecture on the Papacy delivered before the Catholic Truth Society in Oakland, California, undated, Yorke Collection, AUSF.

[59] The Leader, May 7, 1904; Sept. 2, 1911.

[60] Ibid., Feb. 28, 1903.

[61] Everett Carter, "Cultural History Written with Lightning: The Significance of The Birth of a Nation," American Quarterly, XII (Fall, 1960), pp. 347-57.

[62] The Leader, Aug. 2, 1902.

[63] Ibid., Feb. 20, 1904.

[64] Ibid., Dec. 18, 1909. For variations see March 7, 1908, and March 19, 1910.

[65] Ibid., Nov. 3, 1906.

[66] Ibid., Nov. 23, 1907.

[67] Ibid., Dec. 1, 1906.

[68] W. J. Cash, The Mind of the South (New York: Vintage, 1941), pp. 117-20.

[69] The Leader, Dec. 1, 1906.

[70] Loc. cit.

[71] Ibid, July 9, 1904.

[72] Bean, op. cit., pp. 241-3.

[73] The Leader, July 6, 1907.

[74] Brother Leo, "Father Yorke in the Pulpit," The Moraga Quarterly, II (Fall, 1931), p.40.

[75] Bean, op.cit., pp. 13-4.

[76] United States Census Office, op.cit., I, 565.

[77] Brother Matthew McDevitt, The Early Years of St. Mary's College (1859-1879) (mimeographed, undated), p.74.

[78] Edward M. Levine, The Irish and Irish Politicians: A Study of Cultural and Social Alienation (Notre Dame: University of Notre Dame, 1966), p.169.

[79] Oscar Handlin, Al Smith and His America (Boston: Little, Brown, 1956), pp. 171-2, 177.

[80] Brusher, "Peter C. Yorke and the A.P.A. . . . ," p. 144.

[81] "The Sunset Diary, 1900," Yorke Collection, AUSF.

[82] Note Book, No. 18902, Yorke Collection, AUSF.

[83] Peter C. Yorke to Macmillan Co., San Francisco, Oct. 18, 1923; Yorke to Thomas Baker, San Francisco, April 23, 1923. See also Yorke's Diary excerpts, Sept. 24, 1922, all in Yorke Collection, AUSF.

[84] "Paten Book," pp. 57-71, Yorke Collection, AUSF.

[85] P. C. Yorke, Sermons (San Francisco: Text Book Publishing, 1931), I, 181-4.

[86] Ibid., p. 195.

[87] Earlier during his A.P.A. lectures Yorke occasionally cast his antagonists in the roles of scholars, although they hardly qualified. He would then turn on them with anti-intellectual thrusts. His Irish-Catholic-labor following reacted with laughter and applause. See transcript copy of "The Dragon's Teeth," pp. 19, 22, a lecture delivered on April 23, 1896, Yorke Collection, AUSF.

[88] This brand of anti-intellectualism was hardly original with Yorke. See Richard Hofstadter, Anti-Intellectualism in American Life (New York: Vintage, 1962), pp. 151-4.

[89] John Tracy Ellis, The Life of James Cardinal Gibbons: Archbishop of Baltimore, 1834-1921 (Milwaukee: Bruce, 1952), I, 391.

[90] Gaffey, op.cit., pp. 378-80.

[91]Peter E. Hogan, The Catholic University of America, 1896-1903: The Rectorship of Thomas J. Conaty (Washington, D.C.: Catholic University of America, 1949), p. 116.

[92]Ibid., p. 117.

[93]Ibid., pp. 118-9.

[94]Loc. cit.

[95]The Leader, Feb. 22, 1902.

[96]Ibid., Jan. 11, 1902.

[97]Ellis, The Life of James Cardinal Gibbons . . . (Milwaukee: Bruce, 1952), I, 391.

[98]Hogan, op.cit., p.13.

[99]Loc. cit.

[100]Ibid., pp. 168-9.

[101]Gaffey, op.cit., p.342.

[102]The Leader, June 21, 1902.

[103]Ibid., April 26, 1902.

[104]Ibid., June 28, 1902.

[105]Ibid., June 21, 1902.

[106]Loc. cit.

[107]Ibid., August 30, 1902.

[108]Ibid., Feb. 22, 1902.

[109]Ibid., June 28, 1902.

[110]Ibid., Jan. 31, 1903.

[111]Loc. cit.

[112]Ibid., Jan. 24, 1903.

[113] *Loc. cit.*

[114] Ibid., Jan. 31, 1903.

[115] *Loc. cit.*

[116] Ibid., May 30; Jan. 24, 1903.

[117] Ibid., May 30, 1903.

[118] *Loc. cit.*

[119] Ibid., Dec. 12, 1903.

[120] Ibid., July 30, 1904; Aug. 26, 1911; Aug. 17, 1907.

[121] Ibid., Aug. 1, 1908.

[122] Ibid., Jan. 31, 1903.

[123] Ibid., Nov. 1907.

[124] *Loc cit.*

[125] Ibid., Feb. 28, 1903.

[126] *Loc. cit.*

[127] Ibid., Oct. 20, 1906.

[128] Ibid., Dec. 1, 1906.

[129] Ibid., July 29, 1911.

[130] Ibid., Mar. 12, 1910.

[131] Ibid., Aug. 12, 1911, an editorial reprint from the Chicago *New World.*

[132] See *The Leader,* September 23, 1911.

[133] Gaffey, op.cit., pp. 418-9.

[134] P. C. Yorke to J. Harrington, draft, San Francisco, Oct. 15, 1909, Yorke Collection, AUSF.

[135] For a single example see his editorial in *The Leader,* May 10, 1902.

[136] Ibid., Dec. 26, 1903.

[137] Ibid., Nov. 24, 1906; Dec. 26, 1903; Oct. 4, 1902.

[138] Dooley, a talkative Irish saloon-keeper who discussed current affairs with his patrons, had been created by Finley Peter Dunne in 1893. For more on both see William V. Shannon, The American Irish (rev. ed.; New York: Macmillan, 1966), pp. 145-50.

[139] The Leader, June 8, 1908.

[140] Ibid., Aug. 24; Sept. 7, 1907.

[141] Ibid., Feb. 16, 1907.

[142] Ibid., Mar. 9, 1907.

[143] L. Jesse Lemisch, ed., Benjamin Franklin: The Autobiography and Other Writings (New York: New American Library, 1961), p. 226.

[144] See page 28.

[145] Peter C. Yorke, "The Dragon's Teeth," transcript copy, April 23, 1896, Yorke Collection, AUSF.

[146] Stanley M. Elkins, Slavery: A Problem in American Institutional and Intellectual Life (Universal Library ed.; New York: Grosset & Dunlap, 1963), pp. 68-74. Yorke of course was without the benefits of the remarkable volume of literature produced through the twentieth century and still being produced on this subject.

[147] Peter C. Yorke, "The Dragon's Teeth," transcript copy, April 23, 1896, p. 16, Yorke Collection, AUSF.

[148] Ibid., p. 20.

[149] Loc. cit.

[150] Ibid., p. 19.

[151] Elkins, op. cit., pp. 68-72; Frank Tannenbaum, Slave and Citizen: The Negro in the Americas (New York, Vintage, 1946), pp. 62-5.

[152] Hubert Herring, A. History of Latin America (2nd ed. rev.; New York, Knopf, 1964), p. 175.

CHAPTER III

THE APPOINTMENT OF A UNIVERSITY REGENT

The only institution of higher education toward which Yorke overtly expressed any fondness was St. Mary's College. Conducted by the Christian Brothers as a liberal arts college for young men, it was then located in Oakland, later to be moved to Morage. The college was an outgrowth of diocesan efforts rather than the handiwork of the Society of Jesus which was prominent locally. The warm feelings Yorke felt for St. Mary's undoubtedly were not entirely unrelated to the degree of Irish influence through the institution's development to that time. Money needed for its establishment had been collected among Irish miners in early California. The Christian Brothers obtained by Archbishop Alemany, Riordan's predecessor, to teach and administer the college were predominantly Irish.[1] The President of St. Mary's in 1900, Brother Erminold (Charles A. O'Donnell) was born in Limerick.[2] The college's most illustrious faculty member, Brother Leo, was born in Yorke's Irish parish, St. Peter's, and came to maturity under Yorke's spell.[3] With this bond of commonality, Yorke's love for St. Mary's is understandable. The affection was reciprocated. The Brothers granted Yorke a St. Mary's scholarship which he conferred on boys of his choice.[4]

The Regents Under Fire

The occasion which provoked Yorke's appointment as a Regent of the University of California was intimately tied to his fondness for St. Mary's College. The decade of the 1890's had been one of quickening activity within higher education in the Bay Area. Stanford was new, growing and wealthy. In David Starr Jordan it had a president who was articulate and forceful in promoting the destinies of his institution. In 1899 the University of California obtained in Benjamin Ide Wheeler a president who was to preside over the transition of the University. During his years a small state institution serving the local community became one of national and even international renown. Stanford's student body exceeded 1,000 by the mid-nineties and by the turn of the century, Berkeley's exceeded 2,500.[5] Both institutions were growing and both had aggressive presidents. St. Mary's College antedated Stanford by almost a generation and could trace its direct antecedents back almost as far as the University of California. Without state support, or a private fortune comparable to Stanford's, St. Mary's managed as best it could, abundant only in zeal and sacrifice.[6]

By 1900, the Brothers' labors were blessed with a graduating class of fifteen students. On commencement night the youthful graduates gathered with the Brothers, relatives, and friends in a rented Oakland theater to receive their degrees. Their thinness of numbers in no way dampened the ardor of their baccalaureate speaker, however.

For the occasion, Father Yorke had agreed to address the class and issue its members their final charge. Where Yorke went, so went reporters in 1900. His speech was well covered in the San Francisco and Oakland papers the next day, at least in terms of the number of columns devoted to Yorke at St. Mary's.[7] Four days later, however, Yorke felt compelled to set straight the record of what he considered inaccurate reporting. He did so in a series of short articles published in the San Francisco Call.[8]

A synthesis of the original press accounts suggest that Yorke primarily defended the reputations of small colleges against what he believed to be monopolistic mouthings of Jordan and Wheeler. The president and faculty of the University of California, were, in Yorke's estimation, overpaid and undertalented.[9] On this occasion, as on so many others, Yorke maintained he was not the instigator of controversy, but just rising to the open provocations of others. Jordan and Wheeler were attempting, he maintained, to monopolize higher education in California so as to control the public schools as Standard Oil controlled business.[10] His restatement of his views in more clarified form dwelt on the same themes. Yorke felt the teaching staff of St. Mary's was most likely superior to those at California and Stanford. The celibate Brothers were not in university teaching for the money or prestige.[11]

The heart of Yorke's message concerned the State University, its Board of Regents, and its alleged anti-Catholicism. He was apprehensive about the growing influence of the State University over the public and private schools of California. Admission requirements of the State University were influencing the educational offerings at lower levels and served to limit options. And if Berkeley assumed the role of educational guardian in California, he asked who was to watch Berkeley?[12] To Yorke the Board of Regents was not a satisfactory answer since its membership was not representative of the various populations and interests of the state. In fact only lawyers and capitalists served on the Board. More specifically than that, these lawyers and capitalists were not Catholics.

Yorke roughly estimated the Catholic percentage of the state's population and then applied the figure to both the number of Regents and faculty members at Berkeley. He then concluded, "If the Regents were divided in religious belief as is the population of California, there should be six or seven Catholics" on the Board,[13] but prior to 1898 there had been none.[14]

Yorke's explanation for there being only one Catholic Regent and only one Catholic professor was simple religious discrimination. He granted that neither should be selected because of their religious qualification, but argued a representative number of Catholics would have been selected through the natural dynamics of things unless some disturbing variable intervened. Yorke denied that the expertise deemed necessary for Regents and professors was unavailable in the Catholic sector of the state's population. He cited San Francisco as an example where a religious census of the professions -- law, medicine, business, teaching -- would closely approximate the religious affiliations of the population at large.[15] The intervening factor then at Berkeley, clearly, was religious discrimination. And until Catholics were represented at Berkeley they would continue to have little confidence in the institution and its administration and teaching staff. Yorke vociferously maintained that no statements denying discrimination at Berkeley would suffice. The Catholic population of the state simply was not reflected in the composition of the Regents nor in the faculty. "The facts are there and facts are most persuasive."[16]

The Politics of California Higher Education

This may have been the first open attack on the Regents of the University of California by a partisan leader of an ethnic-religious group of the state. Yorke's attack on the Regents was not the first time the Regents were involved in the political arena. By contemporary standards Yorke was even nonpartisan. From 1883 to 1918 the appointments of individual Regents were deeply involved in the state's partisan political controversies. The original system by which Regents were appointed functioned in such a way that their individual terms were staggered so that the sixteen year terms of two Regents expired on each even numbered year. It so happened that these years frequently were election years in California and years in which the State Senate did not meet. And until 1918, the consent of the Senate was required for confirmation of the Governor's appointments to the Board of Regents. Appointments and confirmations ran smoothly until 1883, when the Democratic Party assumed sole control over the governorship and both houses of the state legislature. In their pre-session party caucus they announced that the appointments made by the lame duck Republican Governor would not be confirmed by the Senate. At that time three recent Republican appointees had been serving as Regents awaiting Senate confirmation. Two resigned and the third, Leland Stanford, the ex-Republican Governor of Civil War days, had his name removed from Senate consideration by the new Democratic Governor. James Phelan seems to have been a Democratic victim of the same maneuver in 1899.[17] In 1918 an amendment to the state constitution abolished the requirements of Senate approval. For thirty-five years the change of party control within California placed the appointments of Regents in the balance.[18]

The fact of Yorke's pointed attack on the University of California in 1900 is only part of the story behind his appointment to the Board of Regents two years thereafter. It is the lesser part, at that. Anyone could challenge the way the State University was being managed, but only Yorke bears the distinction of being the critic who possessed sufficient political connections to prompt such an appointment. Because of his colorful battle with the threatening American Protective Association, one which appeared to end in total victory for Catholicism, Yorke became a highly influential personality within his San Francisco subculture. The size of that subculture, added to its traditional facility for political activity, contributed to his importance in public matters of the day. As the popular champion of the Irish, one who enjoyed political combat but because of his clerical calling could not seek office himself, he became a point or orientation around which politicians were well advised to tread lightly. In spite of his Archbishop's strong disapproval, Yorke remained constantly embroiled in municipal politics.[19] It was the result of these political jousts which ultimately provided him with a seat on the Board of Regents.

The year 1896 had been an important one for the creation of Yorke's reputation as a public man. That year marked the end of the American Protective Association in

San Francisco. Yorke cowed their spokesmen into silence or drove them away to more sympathetic environs. In November Yorke's candidate for mayor, Irish-Catholic James Phelan, captured City Hall.[20]

Father Yorke's triumph may have been sweet indeed, but its flavor lingered not for long. James Phelan was as well educated as Yorke, affluent, independent and secure. He favored city charter reforms and must be included within the camp of the Progressives. He was a world traveler, literary dilettante, and general _bon_ _vivant_. He saw life not from Yorke's working-class vantage point, and always had the extra option in life that if issues were not settled to his satisfaction, he need not accept rival solutions at all. His personal wealth and stature allowed him this independence, and in later years, he could withdraw to the grandeur of his Saratoga villa, Montalvo, and allow a foolish world to take a few spins.

Phelan was not a man Yorke could dominate, nor could their respective temperaments and perspectives allow them to travel for long the same course independently. Yorke's relationship with Phelan was a variant of the one with Archbishop Riordan. Both degenerated from active cooperation to conflict. In Phelan's case there was no coexistance. A value towards which Yorke and his Irish subculture attached themselves was the permanency of their priesthood, being a priest then meant forever. Yorke could scrimmage with his Archbishop, but he could not renounce him and his ultimate allegiance to him. To do so was beyond the subculturally imposed options available to Yorke, and quite likely he never thought of such a step. The result was his continued allegiance to a local institution headed by Riordan during the latter's lifetime.

This was not the case with regard to James Phelan, mayor, senator, and social symbol. What started in mutual cooperation never seems to have passed through coexistence but turned quickly to conflict, ripened into vulgarity, only to die in the malice of old age.[21] The initial split between the two politicos came during Phelan's first municipal administration and related to Yorke's central concern, the A.P.A. During his term of office a lease for the Sailor's Home came up for renewal. The home was not a public institution but it was constructed on city property. Yorke considered its management to be under the direction of Protestant sectarianism. Fresh from his tilt with the American Protective Association, he labeled the home, A.P.A. tainted, and opposed renewal. After much inaction the San Francisco Board of Supervisors renewed the lease and Mayor Phelan approved their action. Both Phelan and Dr. C. L. Clinton, a leader on the Board, were Catholics, nonetheless. Yorke denounced them as "Judases" who bowed to bigotry.[22]

As the election of 1898 approached, Yorke publicly and with his usual vigor opposed Clinton and Phelan for re-election. He was determined that both be unseated. Immersing himself in politics, he cast Phelan in the role of the A.P.A. of 1896, a panderer after the votes of bigots. For not denouncing the action of the Supervisors regarding the Sailor's Home, he lost all claim on decent votes. Yorke felt that:

James D. Phelan stands to-day in the forefront of bigotry and intolerance . . . . James D. Phelan is a moral coward, and he is afraid to be a man, because he is afraid of losing votes.[23]

Yorke's letter to the editor of the _Call_, three full columns in length, descended to personal vindictiveness, only to end by denying the same and wallowing in self-justification.

I am not in this matter for personal reasons, and most emphatically I am not in it for politics. If I were anxious for my personal comfort, for the friendship of the rich, for my peace of mind, I would have left town quietly . . . . Perhaps it would have been policy for me to have done so, but God forbid that the day shall ever come when I shall mislead the people that trusted my word and made sacrifices in my cause for the sake of my own peace or for consideration of policy. Principle belongs to men; policy is the watchword of cowards.[24]

Yorke's involvement in the election of 1898 was not limited to city posts. Before the campaign ended he thoroughly embroiled himself in state politics. And this embroilment, more than his St. Mary's assault on the University of California, provided for his appointment as a Regent. The two leading candidates for Governor were Henry T. Gage and James G. Maguire. Gage was a Republican corporation lawyer from Los Angeles. Maguire was a liberal Democratic Congressman from San Francisco. Maguire chose the unfortunate tactic of placing Supervisor Clinton on his campaign committee. Yorke already opposed Clinton's bid for re-election because of the Sailor's Home embroilment. He then opposed Maguire for Governor of California because of his association with Clinton. Yorke's chain of logic traveled from the A.P.A. tainted Sailor's Home, to Clinton's role in the re-leasing, to his support of Maguire. Yorke's conclusion: James G. Maguire was a bigot too.

Yorke had other reasons to question Maguire's religious orthodoxy. Ten years earlier Maguire had published an interesting volume, entitled _Ireland and the Pope_, in which he maintained Ireland was denied its freedom not by English armies, but rather papal intrigues. Yorke's familiarity with the work dated back to the A.P.A. controversy when his antagonists quoted Maguire in support of their anti-popery assertions.[25] During the statewide campaign, Maguire advocated "liberal support" for the University of California, "continuance and improvement of the State text book system," and direct legislation by the people, similar to the referendum later advocated by the Progressives.[26] Yorke opposed all of these as well.

The A.P.A. was, as far as Yorke was concerned, still a live issue in 1898, and he discussed it in person with candidate Maguire. He maintained that Maguire, in private conversation with him, had admitted that Clinton stood for the denial of equal rights to Catholics and promised to remove Clinton from his campaign committee. When he failed to act on this promist, Yorke branded him as "not man enough to stand with those who have since he was able to walk put bread in his stomach and clothes on his back." "False to your father's people, false to your mother's creed, you needed but this crowing infamy, James G. Maguire, that you should be false to your own pledged word."[27] Such was Yorke's public evaluation of the regular Democratic candidate for Governor.

51

Henry T. Gage, the Republican, was a personal friend of Yorke.[28] Four years before this campaign at a Republican covention in Los Angeles, he denounced an A.P.A. resolution only to be hooted off the floor. That was while the A.P.A. was growing, before Yorke had been unleashed by his Archbishop. Because of his early, lone stand against bigotry, Yorke was attracted to Gage as a man of conviction, courage and decency. Yorke recommended him, as such, to Irish-Catholic-labor over Maguire, the renegade.[29] Yorke first delivered the blast in an Oakland speech. To insure maximum coverage, news was leaked to the press that he would publicly denounce the Democrats Maguire and Phelan. Since prereleases were not yet in vogue, newspapers had their shorthand reporters in attendance. The same anti-Democratic content was later distributed as a Gage campaign circular entitled, "Father Yorke to Mr. Maguire."

The reasons for Gage's electoral success were multiple. George Mowry cites the backing of the Southern Pacific, a dominating force in California politics of the day.[30] Melendy and Gilbert list national influences such as the defeat of Spain, President William McKinley's Republican prosperity, and the return of silver Republicans to their party. Yorke's appeal to his subculture to vote against the nominee of the State Democratic Convention was also significant.[31] Under normal conditions, Maguire would have been their candidate. Whatever the root causes for voter behavior on this occasion, the candidates recognized Yorke as a force in politics. Phelan managed to squeak by in a close election while Maguire and Supervisor Clinton were both defeated. Both blamed Yorke for their defeat.[32]

Essentially Yorke was a political man. On most occasions he was the voice of opposition, nipping at the heals of incumbents or clawing at their throats. His championship of James Phelan and his election, back in 1896, did not advance Yorke's interests by his own standard, since Phelan went his own way once in City Hall. As governor, Gage was different, however. He consulted with Yorke concerning San Francisco labor disorder in 1901 and followed his advice.[33] Gage did more than that. He had a reputation for rewarding his friends and party workers with patronage appointments for their loyal political services.[34] In Yorke's case, Governor Gage appointed him a Regent of the University of California. By this political act, Gage provided Yorke his first and only opportunity to operate on a larger stage, one beyond the confines of his own subculture.[35]

The Governor's Reaction

Governor Gage reacted slowly to the charges of religious prejudice levied by his personal friend and political supporter, Father Yorke in 1900. Yorke was a controversial public figure and Gage, wishing a successful administration and renomination, acted with caution. His first move was prompted by the death of Regent Stephen M. White, an ex-United States Senator and the only Catholic on the Board at that time. On March 28, 1901, the Governor appointed in his place an Irish-Catholic attorney and a Democrat, Garret W. McEnerney.[36] Under the current circumstances, or any other for that matter, McEnerney was an ideal selection. This thirty-six year old widower was an alumnus of St. Mary's College and well respected in the legal profession of the city. By all standards he was a success.[37] The following year he was to accompany Archbishop

Riordan to the Hague to win the first case submitted to the Permanent Court of Arbitration, a judgement totaling a million and a half dollars for his Archbishop and the Catholic bishops of California.[38] McEnerney's fee of $10,000 was gladly agreed to by the Archbishop, even when it caused bitter feelings between himself and John T. Doyle, whom McEnerney succeeded as attorney for the Catholic Church.[39]

Gage chose well from the political standpoint, too. McEnerney could symbolically represent St. Mary's and the other small colleges that Yorke felt were being discriminated against, along with Catholics at large. Gage happily accepted their political support in 1889, and he rewarded his supporters.[40] On more general grounds, Gage chose well also. McEnerney had local prestige, was a man of obvious talent, and was on the verge of an expanded career. Above all, McEnerney was on public record as being a firm advocate of higher education. As early as 1895, in a rare interview with a Bulletin reporter, he noted his own St. Mary's experience, and strongly supported the idea of a college education. Self-made men of the past could have done even better had they been better educated, and a college education was the route to professional status.[41] McEnerney possessed, in abundance, all the attributes of those usually selected as Regents, plus the peculiar political prerequisite of the day. He was an Irish-Catholic alumnus of St. Mary's College. And for those who saw the subculture as monolithic, an Irish-Catholic was an Irish-Catholic and by definition was representative. He was not Yorke, though!

Gage's four years as Governor presented him with ample opportunity to reward his friends with place and honor. Not since the creation of the original twenty-two member Board in 1868, had there been so many openings to be filled. During the years of his governorship a record twenty-two new Regents were appointed. The mortality rate among Regents was unusually high and at the end of his term, five of his last eight Regent appointments were to fill the unexpired terms of those who did not live to fulfill their sixteen year terms.

Gage's last appointment to the Board of Regents, executed only after not being renominated by the Republican party and just prior to leaving office, was his old and trusted friend, his political supporter and labor advisor, Father Yorke. All of Gage's final appointments were consented to by the next Senate, meeting in 1903. On February 6, the Senate approved the recommendation of the Committee on Executive Communications. With thirty-one votes being cast, McEnerney received them all with no negatives. Of the six appointments voted on that day, only Yorke received "no" votes but was confirmed, nonetheless, twenty-seven to four.[42]

Father Yorke became a Regent of the University of California at a time when he was known, among other things, as a critic of the University and a personal and political friend of the Governor.

[1]Brother Matthew McDevitt, The Early Years of St. Mary's College (1859-1879) (mimeographed, undated), pp. 8, 42, 56, 61-3, 69.

[2]The Leader, Nov. 15, 1902.

[3]Brother Leo to P. C. Yorke, Moraga, May 23, 1917, Yorke Collection, AUSF; Brother Leo, "Father Yorke in the Pulpit," The Moraga Quarterly, II (Fall, 1931), p. 31.

[4]Peter C. Yorke to Brother Gregory, San Francisco, Aug. 18, 1923, Yorke Collection, AUSF.

[5]John W. Caughey, California (2nd ed.; Englewood Cliffs: Prentice-Hall, 1960), p. 445; Verne A. Stadtman, ed., The Centennial Record of the University of California (Berkeley: University of California, 1967), pp. 216-7.

[6]McDevitt, op. cit., p. 86.

[7]Chronicle (San Francisco), May 25, 1900; Examiner (San Francisco), May 25, 1900; Enquirer (Oakland), May 25, 1900; The Monitor (San Francisco), June 2, 1900.

[8]Peter C. Yorke, Educational Lectures (San Francisco: Text Book Publishing, 1933), pp. 252-3.

[9]Enquirer, May 26, 1900; Chronicle, May 26, 1900.

[10]Examiner, May 26, 1900.

[11]Yorke, Educational Lectures, p. 256.

[12]Ibid., p. 265.

[13]Ibid., pp. 268-9.

[14]On this last point Yorke was slightly inaccurate. John Thomas Doyle (1868-72) was a member of the original Board. Stephen Mallory White (1887-91 and 1899-1901) served as an ex-officio Regent prior to his appointment contemporary to Yorke's St. Mary's speech. James D. Phelan, having never been confirmed by the Senate (1898-99) served briefly, then resigned. Over the years these amounted to less than three percent. Yorke, while not being mathematically exact, did have a very slight margin of error.

[15]Yorke undoubtedly had a point, considering the few Catholics at Berkeley. He dealt from strength with his San Francisco analogy. Law, next to teaching, was among

the professions most easily entered by the working class, and like politics and the church, it strongly attracted talented Irishmen. Business as a profession has many levels from salesclerk to corporate executive. Unlike their Eastern cousins, the Irish arrived in San Francisco before there was a solid establishment and seem to have done better in the business world than Irish elsewhere. Catholics are not noted, however, for general business leadership. See William Miller, "American Historians and the Business Elite," The Journal of Economic History, IX (Nov., 1949). Ireland had an established medical profession was encouraged by the cultural surroundings in America. Yorke did not mention science or other areas of intellectual achievement, areas from which university types are often drawn. In these fields the Catholic record has been poor indeed, considering the number of Catholics in America. See John Tracy Ellis, American Catholics and the Intellectual Life (Chicago: Heritage Foundation, 1956).

[16] Yorke, Educational Lectures, p.271.

[17] William Carey Jones, Illustrated History of the University of California (rev. ed.; Berkeley: Student's Cooperative Society, 1901), p.385.

[18] Stadtman, op.cit., p. 404.

[19] James P. Gaffey, The Life of Patrick William Riordan: Second Archbishop of San Francisco, 1841-1914 (Ph.D. dissertation, Catholic University of America, 1965), p. 418.

[20] Joseph S. Brusher, S.J., "Peter C. Yorke and the A.P.A. in San Francisco," The Catholic Historical Review, XXXVII (July, 1951), pp. 149-50.

[21] The Leader, March 14, 1908; James D. Phelan to editor of the Irish World (New York), February 29, 1924, Phelan MSS, Bancroft Library, Berkeley.

[22] Gaffey, op.cit., p.405.

[23] Examiner, (San Francisco), Nov. 1, 1898.

[24] Call (San Francisco), Nov. 2, 1898.

[25] Gaffey, op.cit., p.408.

[26] James G. Maguire, "Issues of the Campaign of 1898," Sept. 14, 1898, Yorke Collection, AUSF.

[27] Peter C. Yorke, "Father Yorke to Mr. Maguire," pamphlet, Yorke Collection, AUSF.

[28] Howard Brett Melendy and Benjamin F. Gilbert, Governors of California: Peter H. Burnett to Edmund G. Brown (Georgetown, Calif.: Talisman, 1965), p.268.

[29] *Examiner*, Nov. 1, 1898.

[30] George E. Mowry, *The California Progressives* (Chicago: Quadrangle, 1963), p. 16.

[31] Melendy and Gilbert, op.cit., p.263.

[32] *Bulletin* (San Francisco), Dec. 14, 1898; *Call* (San Francisco), Nov. 27, 1898.

[33] Melendy and Gilbert, op.cit., p.268.

[34] *Loc. cit.*

[35] Years later in the midst of a white-hot exchange with Yorke, the Editor of the *Sacramento Bee*, Charles K. McClatchy, called Yorke's support of Gage "prearranged probably prepaid. And after the election Gage did not forget his ally . . . . If it were . . . proper that a Roman Catholic priest should be on the Board of Regents, it would have been little enough to ask that the Governor should at least pick out an honest one." McClatchy was a Catholic. *Sacramento Bee*, Dec. 10, 1908.

[36] *The Journal of the Senate, Legislature of the State of California*, 35th Session, 1903, p.16.

[37] Oscar T. Shuck, *History of the Bench and Bar of California* (Los Angeles: Commercial Printing House, 1901), pp. 638-41.

[38] Garret W. McEnerney, "Pious Fund of the Californias," *The Catholic Encyclopedia* XII (1913), pp. 106-7.

[39] Gaffey, op.cit., pp. 352, 354; William E. McDonald, "The Pious Fund of the Californias," *The Catholic Historical Review*, XIX (Jan., 1934), p. 435.

[40] Melendy and Gilbert, op.cit., p. 268.

[41] Shuck, op.cit., p. 638.

[42] *The Journal of the Senate, Legislature of the State of California* 35th Session, 1903, pp. 16, 320, 344-5.

CHAPTER IV

THE UNIVERSITY OF CALIFORNIA, 1900-1912

Early Congregational Influence

The State University which Yorke attacked with such vigor in 1900 sprang from origins not too dissimilar from his own beloved St. Mary's. The University of California was a direct descendant of the College of California, an institution created by deep religious fervor. St. Mary's resulted from the cooperation between the Christian Brothers and the Archbishop of San Francisco and was supported by the local Catholic population. Its early history is heavily laden with personal sacrifice and zeal, but sparse material resources.[1]

The driving force behind the College of California, the individual later to become the first president of the State University, was a man of the cloth too, Henry Durant.[2] A graduate of Yale and its theological seminary, Durant spent thirteen years as Pastor of the Congregational Church at Byfield, Massachusetts, and then sailed for California, arriving in 1853. This relocation followed a three year hiatus as head of a Byfield academy. Durant quickly presented his educational scheme to the annual meeting of the Congregational Association and the Presbytery of the New School Presbyterian Church, which immediately appointed four ministers to assist him in bringing his dreams to fruition.[3]

The new College of California, officially non-denominational, was totally immersed in Congregationalism.[4] Durant retained his ministerial standing until 1869, severing his official connection, not as a result of growing disinterest in religious affairs, but rather because of very intense religious conviction.[5] The College's Board of Trustees similarly reflected, in its membership, the influence given to Protestantism.[6]

The College of California differed in one very significant way from St. Mary's in its response to the problems of growth and development. Aspirations of the Trustees for their college far outdistanced available private funds. Their hope for public moneys died when the California legislature responded to the Morrill Land Grant Act by authorizing a public institution of higher education, which it located adjacent to College of California property in Berkeley. At this point, the Trustees, rather than curtailing their educational goals, instead voted to donate all their property to the state, insisting, however, that a university be created with instruction not being confined merely to the minimum requirements of the Morrill Act.[7] This done, the old College of California disincorporated and was absorbed into the new State University.

Beyond the presence of Durant, tangible proof of continued Congregational influence over the University of California during its early years is a bit difficult to posit. While waning, it did continue to exist. Reverend Horatio Stebbins, Thomas Starr King's successor as pastor of San Francisco's Unitarian Church, was the only hold-over from the College's Trustees to the Regents of the University of California. Reverend J. Harmon C. Bonté, an Episcopal minister, served as Secretary of the Regents, Superintendent of Grounds, and Secretary of the Academic Senate.[8] In addition to these well-placed and, in the case of the latter two, persisting figures, faculty from the College of California had also been absorbed into the University. An outstanding example was Martin Kellogg. As a Congregational clergyman, he joined the faculty of the College of California in 1859. When it was absorbed into the State University, he was appointed professor of Latin and Greek and continued to teach almost to the time of his death in 1903. During the decade of the 1890's he served as President of the University and vacated the office upon the arrival of Benjamin Ide Wheeler. George Holmes Howison came to Berkeley in 1884, as Professor of Moral and Intellectual Philosophy. Howison had forsaken the ministry after attending Lane Theological Seminary.[9]

This Congregational influence upon the University, rather than being quasi-conspiratorial in nature, seems more a mere reflection of what at the time was central in American society at large, a pervasive influence which manifested itself in education, particularly. As the years passed and society became more secular, this too was reflected in the University. A first step seems to have been a gravitation on the part of preacher's sons to teaching at the University, but their break with family traditions was far from complete, as evidenced by their periodic occupation of Berkeley pulpits.[10]

A New President Builds a New Faculty

At the turn of the century, many faculty undoubtedly were as comfortable in a pulpit as they were behind a lectern. President Benjamin Ide Wheeler, a minister's son married to a minister's daughter, was one, as was Charles Mills Gayley, head of the English department, who also shared identical clerical connections.[11] But by 1900, the University had grown far beyond the various limitations surrounding its birth and early development, and was in fact on the threshold of becoming a modern University in competition with the long established higher educational institutions of the East. The faculty had grown from the original ten members at Berkeley in 1868, to 207 University-wide by 1900. Within the next dozen years the number was to rise to an even 400.[12]

During this period the scientific attainments of the University faculty were recognized by the prizes of foreign academies, while the University's special equipment was sought after by Eastern universities for their experimental undertakings.[13] Professors received appointments to federal boards which related to areas within their range of academic specialization. They delivered foreign lectures by appointment and at least one professor was requested to stop at the White House for debriefing following his proposed trip to the Russian borderlands.[14] Another, a young zoologist, was invited by Theodore Roosevelt to accompany him on his famous post-presidential

African expedition.[15]

As a condition for accepting the Presidency of the University of California, Benjamin Ide Wheeler had insisted that he have charge of the direction of all University employees, including their appointments, removals and salaries.[16] Once the Regents of the University of California agreed to Wheeler's conditions for accepting the Presidency, they assumed for themselves a supporting role in the direction of the institution, a condition which they probably preferred, and one which did advance the interests of higher education under state auspices. As long as Wheeler's mode of operation remained in vogue, the University prospered under his close management. When the spirit of the times moved on to a more advanced position, which included faculty participation in the institutional decision making process, Wheeler was dethroned by the faculty, provided a position of respect and dignity, and ignored.[17] After that the institution continued under new leadership, haltingly for a while, but adjustment was made. The period from 1900 to 1912 were years during which Wheeler was the undisputed ruler of the campus. The organizational structure was definitely hierarchical and he headed the hierarchy.[18] During these years the Regents generally responded to his proposals and worked to support his dreams and innovations for the University.

When they chose Wheeler in 1899, they chose well. At the age of forty-five he was at the peak of his scholarly life. One might say his scholarly work came to fulfillment at the very moment he left Cornell for California, or probably more accurately, it was terminated by accepting a university presidency. At any rate, his important publications preceded his California experience.[19]

In the preliminary sparring between Professor Wheeler and the Regents of the University concerning the presidency, Wheeler negotiated from a position of security. In 1899 Berkeley was a very local institution, and seen from the Ivy League, it probably seemed to be located somewhere between the Great American Desert and Samoa. Certainly the University had great possibilities which might be actualized, but risks existed, too. Before the turn of the century, a scholar coming to California chanced intellectual suicide at worst, a knowledge gap at best.[20] For an administrator, acceptance of such a call might mean virtual banishment. Wheeler recognized this and drove a demanding bargain. The result was that he became, as he put it, President in fact as well as in theory.[21] He remained such for twenty years while California became a University.

He held the hiring process centralized in his own hands and sought faculty for his expanding institution.[22] During his first year Wheeler crossed the continent more than seven times to locate and interview candidates for his departments.[23]

The President of the University was a man of reputation and stature, but beyond that he had the liberal support of the state and Board of Regents. To attract the quality personnel on which the reputation of the University was to be based, he was able to offer in addition to substantial salaries, at times supplemented by private subsidies, occasional moving allowances of $1000 and appointments which began with European leave.[24] Also during these years a faculty retirement plan gradually evolved. The

President's ability to acquire quality faculty was not perfect, but surely well above average. Occasionally one got away as in the case of W. E. Dodd, the historian and later New Deal diplomat.[25]

Also among the appointees selected by the President were those who were to preside over the various subdivisions of the University. Following the hierarchical concept, Wheeler invariably supported his chairmen in the periodic skirmishing and occasional warfare between members of the instructional staff and the department heads. Through his calculated inaction, personnel decisions made by his department heads stood.[26] There was no appeal process.

The upgrading of the quality of faculty at the University of California during the first dozen years of the twentieth century was not an unmixed blessing. It would seem from the pattern which was established that Berkeley had entered big league musical chairs; offers and counteroffers reverberated from early March. The start of the fall term marking the end of the music. During this period, California sought mostly junior members of prestigeous institutions in the East. The East retaliated by picking off more senior Berkeley men for professorships, endowed chairs, and department headships.[27] Yale, Harvard and the College of the City of New York recruited at Berkeley.[28] Even President Wheeler received offers of three Eastern presidencies; the most attractive being from the Massachusetts Institute of Technology.[29]

Untroubled Students

Students at Berkeley in 1900 were drawn almost entirely from the State of California, and almost all of these were from the northern part of the state. Of the 328 degrees conferred by the University in May 1900, both undergraduate and graduate (academic and professional), only nineteen graduates came from beyond the state and of those, sixteen earned graduate degrees. Of the three undergraduates who hailed from distant parts, one was from Oregon, a second from Ohio, and one resident of Japan was solely responsible for the international composition of the class of 1900.

The University dental and medical schools succeeded better in attracting foreign students. Almost twelve percent of the graduates (6/51) were from beyond North America, the class having a thin sampling from Sweden, Guatemala, England and Japan. But even the professional schools were predominantly serving local needs.[30] Total enrollment at the University of California for the year 1899-1900 was 2,553 with undergraduate students providing the bulk (1,988).[31] At the undergraduate instructional level, Berkeley was exceeded only by Harvard in total numbers among American institutions of higher learning at the beginning of the twentieth century.[32]

The State University was at a point in its institutional development at which personal philanthropy and service were recognized and appreciated by untroubled students. Those who might select this as the golden age of university development would be overwhelmed by student reaction to state support. President Wheeler announced at a student gathering in 1903 that the Governor had just signed a bill authorizing $250,000 for campus construction. Students received the news with wild enthusiasm and vociferously cheered the Governor, the state legislature and the state itself. When Wheeler announced that Governor George C. Pardee would participate in Charter Day exercises, the student body responded with a second round of wild applause for their Governor.[33] Campus disorders were amiable events.[34]

Random information strongly suggests that while a surge towards system, order, efficiency, and bureaucracy was under way, the University and its community were still small, rather close knit and local in orientation. A rather homogeneous population agreed on basic assumptions, and life within this community was lived in relative harmony. Growth and development within the University, as opposed to quiescence, can easily be seen through the administrative reorganizations which took place, necessitated by the trebling of student enrollment and faculty, and by the addition of twenty new departments of instruction through the Wheeler administration.[35] In order to accomplish these reorganizations Wheeler denied himself European leaves, feeling that his personal presence was needed so as to minimize the friction which inevitably results from change in established patterns.[36]

Academic Government

Faculty government always existed at Berkeley, but with varying degrees of virility. During the 1870's and 80's, the faculty Senate was at its weakest point, but in the final decade of the century, individual leadership within a growing and talented faculty began retrieving some of the traditional prerogatives.[37] The appointment of Benjamin I. Wheeler as President in 1899 produced a dual effect on academic government within the University. His transformation of a community oriented college into a university of world renown brought to Berkeley scholars who were among the most talented in their respective fields. It was only inevitable that such men would wish to control their own academic affairs, such tendencies being buttressed by the democratic aspects of the greater environment. In the long run, these developments provided for greater democratization of internal government. But until this future arrived, the atmosphere was stultified and repressive. Wheeler was vigilant to see that no relationship should exist between the faculty and the Regents.[38] All communications from the Academic Senate and individual faculty members to the Regents were to flow through the President's hands. While Wheeler remained President, he suppressed the desires of the faculty for a share, not only in the decision making process, but also in prior consultation and deliberation. The Academic Senate recommended standards for admissions, high school accreditation and some curricular items.[39] But the faculty was denied a voice over such matters as appointments, promotions, budgets, and educational policy, until they were confronted with the decision either to remain quiescent or revolt. They did not choose the latter until 1919.[40]

Financial Stability

The financial history of the University of California has been marked by the continued generosity of the people of the State. Expenditures from the start have been generous and have continued even through periods of economic stress within the state.[41] Throughout the years here being considered, the total operating income always increased.

61

The portion of this income contributed by the state seldom exceeded half of the sum total, yet this state contribution always remained generous and always increased. Even during the year of the great San Francisco earthquake and fire, when much public property was destroyed and the state's general tax base was greatly eroded, support of the University increased in a predictable manner, consistent with past and future years. The University endowment at the turn of the century was a shade under four million dollars and the operating income for the year 1900-01 was $422,000 or about $6,000 more than the total expenditures.[42]

The University endowment compared unfavorably with the older Ivy League institutions and Stanford, yet, state support of the yearly operating budget was always much greater than the annual endowment income. Between 1900 and 1912, all sources of income to the University increased markedly, but the advance in the proportion of the state financial support to endowment income increased over fourfold. If annual state financial support was added to annual endowment income, to obtain such a total income from endowment alone would require an endowment comparable to, or greater than, that enjoyed by Cornell, the University of Chicago, or Yale.[43]

From the outset, President Wheeler vigorously fulfilled the expectations of his new office. The subject of his first commencement address was the financial condition of the University and the need for greater funds in order that California might truly become a University. In 1900, Wheeler pointed out that while the total income available to the University increased 70 percent over the preceding decade, the student population had shot up 370 percent. Placing California in a class with Eastern universities, he claimed they spent a million or more dollars per year on the conduct of education.[44] If such was the case, Chicago, Columbia, and Harvard were exceeding their yearly incomes by about half, one third, and one quarter, respectively.[45] But in any case, Wheeler felt confident that the state would respond by making California one of the world's leading universities.

Wheeler was correct. Public support was marked by generosity consistent with his expectations.[46] During these same years, and not reflected in income disbursement figures, the legislature passed special appropriations for major campus construction,[47] and voters supported massive bond issues. None of these beneficent acts came totally unsolicited. The Regents chose well when they called Wheeler to guide the University to its future. He was attentive to legislative affairs, and during the session he visited the State Capitol frequently, even weekly at times.[48]

As the President endeavored to increase the income, the Regents in these early days worked closely with the modest endowment in order to conserve what was already theirs for the University. The Finance Committee members under Regent Arthur W. Foster managed the endowment not too differently from the way they might manage the capital of their own early banks. Amounts of up to $50,000 were let out at interest to local individuals and secured by real property. Interest varied from five to seven percent per year with from three to five years as the life of the loan. Such undertakings were closely and personally attended to by individual Regents and were characterized by localism and conservatism.[49]

Another major and ever increasing source of University income has, from the start, been private gifts and philanthropy. The largest contributors are now known to even the casual Berkeley visitor through the campus landmarks which bear their names. And with the advent of campus activism, these same names, for a while, became almost household words throughout the nation and wherever activist students met. Little did Jane K. Sather think that the gate memorializing her husband would later be beamed throughout the nation via network television. These thoughts certainly never entered her mind when she corresponded with President Wheeler about the disposition of the property she willed to the University. [50]

Buried beneath these massive contributions to the University are the smaller but much more numerous gifts which have been accepted by the Regents through the years. Many of these lesser sums were substantial in themselves and undoubtedly served to raise morale by providing the unexpected bonus which enriched the learning process by providing the few thousands needed to purchase this rare library of a deceased Berlin professor, or to send that promising young scientist to Egypt or Labrador to observe an eclipse. [51] These were the gifts of the moderately wealthy who paused in their counting houses to consider the values of the intellectual life. Of the $230,000,000 donated to California through its history, few mementos could be more thoughtful than those recorded in the Regent's Minute Book during the early century: the professor's widow contributing his library because "the best and happiest years of his life were spent at the University," the aged scholar verging on emeritus status giving $125 toward a graduate scholarship in memory of his wife and child, and the anonymous young graduate eager about the prospects before her who promised a modest monthly remittance from her first job, a sum which surely would evaporate in the dynamics of the budgetary process. [52]

An Adult Institution

Yes, the University was big and growing in size and complexity. This is evident in its financial affairs and in other ways, from 1900 to 1912. Still these affairs were understandably, could be, and were managed without an impersonal staff of technical experts. Should patterns be reduced to statistical data and traced through the first dozen years of the twentieth century, University life would show constant increase. This is true of dollars, people, square fee, publications, awards, or contacts with eminent personages. In a sense, these years of the Wheeler administration might be characterized as a lift-off point in adult institutional development. Symbolic of this maturation and slow surge into the new century was the comprehensive building plan for the Berkeley campus and its implementation.

This plan originated in 1896 with Mrs. Phoebe Hearst, who functioned in the dual capacity of Regent and interested philanthropist through the middle years of the University's history. Under the general guidance of this comprehensive plan the modern campus of the University emerged. Ground breaking for the first building, the President's House, took place May 12, 1900. The first completed structure, the Greek Theater, was ready for use in the fall of 1903. Other major structures contained within the nucleus of the present day campus include the Hearst Memorial Mining Building,

California Hall, Doe Library, the old Boalt Hall (now Durant Hall), Agriculture Hall, and ultimately Wheeler Hall. These impressive structures were provided by individual philanthropy, special legislative appropriation, publicly supported bond issues, and subscription among interested professional organizations.

By the time Father Peter C. Yorke was lashing out against the University of California, it had already moved away from its Congregational origins and would continue in that direction. At the start of the twentieth century, the University had already attained adult status as an institution. Its talented, energetic, and forceful president was elevating the standards of scholarship, while at the same time expanding and developing a modern, comprehensive University. Public and private support and encouragement of the University was widespread.

The period from 1900 to 1912, the dates between which Yorke concerned himself with University affairs, was a period of well-planned, consistent growth. The very selection of these years for either a still photo or a moving historical picture is awkward at best, because the institution's movement through greater development began before 1900, and the termination of Yorke's Regency marked no turning point in the history of California. When he challenged the administration of the State University before the fifteen St. Mary's graduates of 1900, he challenged those who, though not Irish-Catholics, were talented, honest, and efficient builders of an admirable educational enterprize, one which enjoyed widespread approval and respect.

[1]Brother Matthew McDevitt, The Early Years of St. Mary's College (1859-1879) (mimeographed, undated), pp. 80, 86.

[2]William W. Ferrier, Henry Durant: First President University of California, The New Englander Who Came to California With College on the Brain (Berkeley: private, 1942).

[3]Ibid., pp. 9-13.

[4]Northern California Writers Program of the Work Projects Administration, Berkeley: The First Seventy-Five Years (Berkeley: Gillick Press, 1941), p.52.

[5]Ferrier, op.cit., pp. 95, 134-45.

[6]Northern California Writers, op.cit., p. 26.

[7]Ibid., pp. 40-1; Verne A. Stadtman, ed., The Centennial Record of the University of California (Berkeley: University of California, 1967), pp. 375, 127, 12.

[8]Stadtman, op.cit., p. 405; William Carey Jones, Illustrated History of the University of California (rev. ed.; Berkeley: Student's Cooperative Society, 1901), p. 381. Yorke may well have disliked this arrangement but undoubtedly disapproved even more of Bonté's successor as Secretary of the Regents. He was removed during Yorke's Regency for theft and subsequent Secretaries have been bonded. See Minute Book, XIV, 252, Regents of the University of California, Office of the Secretary of the Regents, Berkeley. Hereafter cited, UC Regent's Minute Book.

[9]Stadtman, op.cit., pp. 14-5; Ferrier, op.cit., p. 468.

[10]Benjamin P. Kurtz, Charles Mills Gayley (Berkeley: University of California, 1943), pp. 127-8; Berkeley Daily Gazette, June 8, July 27, 1908.

[11]Monroe E. Deutsch, ed., The Abundant Life (Berkeley: University of California, 1926), pp. 1-19; Kurtz, op.cit., pp. 12-15, 136.

[12]Stadtman, op.cit., pp. 265, 270, 272.

[13]UC Regent's Minute Book, XVI, 203; XIV, 97.

[14]Ibid., XV, 315; Benjamin I. Wheeler to Lydia M. Chadwick, Berkeley, Aug. 3, 1909, Wheeler manuscripts housed in the Archives of the University of California, Berkeley, hereafter cited, Wheeler MSS AUC. Wheeler to Theodore Roosevelt, Berkeley, May 25, 1903, Wheeler MSS AUC.

[15] Wheeler to Theodore Roosevelt, Berkeley, Oct. 24, 1908, Wheeler MSS AUC.

[16] Wheeler to Martin Kellogg, Wm. T. Wallace, and Henry S. Foot, Ithaca, June 24, 1899, Wheeler MSS AUC. The very wording of the pertinent paragraphs of the Regent's Manual of 1904 is the same as Wheeler's 1899 letter. See UC Regent's Minute Book, XIV, 289.

[17] Stadtman, op.cit., p. 290. On alleged pro-Germanism and the University during World War I see Kurtz, op.cit., pp. 224-9.

[18] Based on interviews with faculty leaders who overthrew Wheeler, Arthur E. Hutson characterized his presidency as "dictatorial." See Hutson, "Faculty Government," in Stadtman, op.cit., p. 290.

[19] Deutsch, op.cit., pp. 1-19; Wheeler to D. C. Heath, Berkeley, Mar. 22, 1900; Wheeler to Charles Scribner, Berkeley, Jan. 9, 1900, Wheeler MSS AUC.

[20] Deutsch, op.cit., p. 32.

[21] Wheeler to Martin Kellogg, Wm. T. Wallace, and Henry S. Foot, Ithaca, June 24, 1899, Wheeler MSS AUC.

[22] UC Regent's Minute Book, XIV, 289.

[23] Wheeler to E. W. Huffcut, Berkeley, Aug. 15, 1900; Wheeler to M. A. Tuxbury, Berkeley, Mar. 14, 1900; Wheeler to Charles A. Kofoid, New York City, June 29, 1900, Wheeler MSS AUC.

[24] UC Regent's Minute Book, XIV, 246, 269; XV, 417.

[25] Ibid., XVI, 59.

[26] Berkeley Daily Gazette, Aug. 26, 1908; UC Regent's Minute Book, XV, 216.

[27] UC Regent's Minute Book, XIV, 332; XV, 232; XVI, 235; Daily Californian, Mar. 10, 1908.

[28] UC Regent's Minute Book, XVI, 8, 79, 243; XV, 306.

[29] Wheeler to Warren Olney, Berkeley, Aug. 8, 1907; Wheeler to A. S. Ide, Berkeley, Aug. 8, 1907, Wheeler MSS AUC.

[30] UC Regent's Minute Book, XII, 35-46.

[31] Stadtman, op.cit., pp. 216-7.

[32] William W. Ferrier, Origin and Development of the University of California (Berkeley: Sather Gate Book Shop, 1930), p. 442.

[33] Daily Californian, March 16, 1903.

[34] Ibid., March 18, 1908.

[35] Stadtman, op.cit., p. 15; UC Regent's Minute Book, XIV, 284, 288; XVI, 275.

[36] Wheeler to A. S. Ide, Berkeley, May 17, 1912, Wheeler MSS AUC.

[37] Stadtman, op.cit., p. 289.

[38] Wheeler to H. B. Lord, Berkeley, Aug. 23, 1900, Wheeler MSS AUC.

[39] UC Regent's Minute Book, XIV, 284-5; XVI, 183, 285.

[40] Stadtman, op.cit., p.290.

[41] Ibid., pp. 293-4.

[42] Ibid., pp. 295-6.

[43] Ferrier, Origin and Development of the University of California, p. 443.

[44] Examiner, May 17, 1900.

[45] Ferrier, Origin and Development of the University of California, p.445.

[46] Stadtman, op.cit., p. 294.

[47] UC Regent's Minute Book, XIV, 81.

[48] Wheeler to Mrs. Herbert Tuttle, Berkeley, Feb. 8, 1907, Wheeler MSS AUC.

[49] UC Regent's Minute Book, XIV, 247, 270, 319, 353. In 1908 the Alameda County Auditor set mortgages held by the University within the county at near one million dollars.

[50] For her letter to Wheeler dated Feb. 10, 1911, see UC Regent's Minute Book XVII, 51.

[51] Ibid., XIV, 241, 258.

[52] Ibid., XIV, 163, 137; XVI, 383.

CHAPTER V

THE UNIVERSITY COMMUNITY ON THE EVE OF PROGRESSIVISM

Community Consensus

Harmony and tranquility are the adjectives which best characterized the relationship between the University of California and the Berkeley community through the first decade of the twentieth century. The town's population, when compared to that of the metropolis across the bay, was homogeneous, and this homogeniety permeated the University. Agreement generally existed on basic assumptions concerning the nature of the good society and how it ought to be constructed. Since the local community seemed quite content to leave the intricacies of the educational process to the University professionals, no reason exists to doubt that this general agreement existed on basic educational assumptions too.

At first glance it might even appear that Regent Yorke would fit easily and comfortably into this set of circumstances. His racial obsession, for example, was not a factor which separated him from the dominant sectors of the Berkeley community. While the blatancy associated with working-class racism was not overt in Berkeley, sufficient manifestations of racism existed within the local press, church, University faculty, and administration to support the generalization that key community components all agreed, whether openly or by quiet sanction, with the basic racial assumptions to which Yorke subscribed.[1]

For most residents of the University town, the question of race was undoubtedly one which interested them, one which could bring to the surface their latent dispositions. Few practical issues arose in their midst, however, which touched the racial question. Berkeleyites could be interested in race, but it was not one of their practical concerns in the first decade of the century. What did concern them was moral or social control of semi-public or private behavior, namely liquor consumption.

The area of contention over which much newsprint was spilt throughout 1908 was demon rum, the corrupter of youth and despoiler of fathers. By state law a one mile limit surrounded the University campus within which the sale of liquor was illegal. The citizens of the town, through their trustees, had proceeded further and had outlawed liquor within the town limits.[2] Legally then, in 1908, Berkeley was a dry town, a situation quite at odds with conditions across the bay in San Francisco. This condition, however, seemed to be heartily approved by the main sectors of the Berkeley citizenry. Opinion, however, was not unanimous and sobriety was ever a troublesom virtue to enforce.[3]

Those who favored total prohibition for Berkeley generally were among those who belonged to civic improvement and booster clubs, were middle or upper-middle class, and may have moved to Berkeley so as to be close to the University where they planned to educate their sons -- an education they ardently wished to be completed without the influence of a local saloon. President Wheeler favored prohibition.[4] Those who opposed it belonged to a very different socio-economic order. The working-class lived on the flat lands west of the Southern Pacific Railroad tracks, and they wanted their liquor in saloons. Exceptions undoubtedly existed but the general conflict over prohibition was between East and West Berkeley, between upper income types and the working-class, between hill dwellers and those on the flats.

Beyond the Consensus

Differences of opinion and clashing modes of behavior relating to prohibition met at the police station, the justice court, and meetings of the town trustees. The personnel running these governmental functions ardently supported prohibition, and responded favorably to the general wishes of the dominant sectors in Berkeley, namely the reform-booster-minded improvement clubs. Protestant church organizations, and University spokesmen. The prominent exception was Trustee William Schmidt from the Westside's Seventh Ward. While hardly a political "boss" in the sense of one who headed an urban "machine," Schmidt was the closest facsimile Berkeley had for the same, and in the minds of the reformers, undoubtedly appeared as a Tweed or Ruef in the midst of aspiring civic virtue. He rejected prohibition and worked for its abolition. In doing so, he advocated the views of his ward and opposed those of the greater part of Berkeley. Considered in the context of the prohibition issue, his views were contained and overruled by an otherwise unanimous consensus; one of course which excluded him and his ward.

This Berkeley consensus included a proliferation of civic betterment clubs containing a clerical base, and academic and business wings. This dominant sector was unable to come to terms with the Seventh Ward and its trustee, and the Westsiders would not be ignored.

The most common method of providing needed public services which had not been budgeted was through bond sales. A two-thirds majority vote of the people, however, was required to authorize such bond issues, and Schmidt's Seventh Ward consistently opposed such measures. Shoreline residents in 1908, halted town garbage collection when they threatened to summarily shoot any scavenger who dumped another wagon load on the bay tidelands near their homes.[5] The alternative chosen by the trustees was to burn the garbage, but the bonds needed for the purchase of an incinerator were voted down by the Seventh Warders.[6] School bonds also went down in defeat, and under opposition from the Westsiders, bonds for rat control were never brought to a vote. Citizens from War Seven tended to think that they were bearing a heavy property tax burden for benefits which went to other sections of town, the foothills and slopes. Ministers, professors, and businessmen were highly influential in civic affairs, but they were unable to control absolutely.

The Reform Impulse

     In the year 1908, Berkeley fully embraced the Progressive Movement,[7] a reform movement which in California was destined to dethrone the Southern Pacific Railroad as the controlling interest in the State's political and economic life. Already Berkeley citizens had been exciting themselves over some of the same type activities which were becoming more voguish through parts of California and in other parts of the United States. In Berkeley during that year the rallying points from which aroused citizens warred on political sin and civic complacency were the neighborhood improvement clubs.[8]

     Closely associated with these civic clubs were Protestant churches of Berkeley. Pastors, officers, and members of congregations attended sermons upstairs and listened to civic improvement speakers in the halls below. One Catholic Church served all Berkeley Catholics, while thirty-seven Protestant churches of varying stances from the more fundamental to liberal dotted the rest of the Berkeley landscape. This situation was quite at odds with prevailing conditions in San Francisco. Through 1908 the press never mentioned St. Joseph's, its pastor, or his young Irish assistants as participants in civic uplift type activities.

     Reform in Berkeley appeared a Protestant perserve. At St. Mark's Episcopal Church an Anti-Race Track League was organized under the auspices of a clergy and professors.[9] The state's leading Progressive of the day, Chester Rowell, was hosted at a Unitarian banquet after which he spoke about political reform. So impressed by his views was the Reverend Edward Lambe Parsons, of St. Mark's, that the next day he sent Rowell a note of appreciation along with one of his own addresses which also treated Rowell's theme.[10] A second honored guest that same evening was Reverend Charles W. Wendte who was introduced in glowing terms for his pioneer ministerial efforts in San Francisco. The master of ceremonies noted that if younger ministers then found the field to be a pleasant one, they could thank Wendte. It was not mentioned that Wendte was the last of Father Peter C. Yorke's antagonists in the American Protective Association controversy of 1896.[11] Wendte, Parsons, and Rowell, like members of the Anti-Race Track League, were devotees of urban reform.

     The most provocative civil development which attracted Berkeley's attention concerned them only indirectly. It was the sensational San Francisco graft prosecutions. Most of the San Francisco supervisors had admitted bribe taking and the district attorney's office, with liberal private backing, was anxious to obtain convictions.[12] As polyglot San Francisco became bored with the seemingly endless series of trials, homogeneous Berkeley quickened to the pace.

     From his Sunday pulpit the Reverend S. D. Hutsinpiller, Pastor of Trinity Methodist Episcopal Church, denounced urban bossism, corruption, and backsliding San Franciscans for forsaking the cause of righteousness. He also stated his support of Francis Heney, the controversial special prosecutor who was directing the graft proceedings.[13] The true test of Berkeley's commitment, though, was passed by the men's club of Bethany Congregational Church. On the evening of June 16, they endured a three hour after-dinner speech by the chief prosecutor, Heney, himself.[14]

Those Berkeleyites who possessed such endurance in behalf of reform shared equivalent views of what the contemporary status of politics and local government was, and also what it ought to be. The state wide figure whom they respected most in this field of activism undoubtedly was Chester Rowell, Editor of the Fresno Republican. Often a welcomed speaker at church-booster dinners, he always received an enthusiastic hearing. While not a Berkeley resident himself, it would not stretch the truth to say Berkeley and he were one in the spirit. Early in his career, in a letter to his father, he told how he found himself active in politics at the local level. It is a letter very revealing of a man who was to rise to prominence in state Progressive reform circles. The views expressed therein were generally shared by Berkeley club-church activists of 1908, the only differences being Rowell expressed them earlier, clearer, and more concisely. About town government and his uncle who declined the nomination for mayor he said in part:

> [Uncle Chester] found he could not accept without resigning his position as Regent of the University [of California] in which he has still ten years to serve, and I found that if I did not accept [,] the nomination would go to a disreputable politician . . . . So I accepted the nomination, on a non-partisan platform, and with a pledge, if elected, to run the city on business principles, without politics. Of course the politicians took these public professions as sure bluff . . . and as soon as I was nominated began to give practical advice as to what I was to do in private. I was to make high professions to get the "church vote," as they call the respectable vote, and then . . . I was to make the rounds of the saloons and brothels and make promises to "protect" them . . . . I was to see the Catholic priest and get him to deliver his votes. I was to see the gamblers and promise not to interfere with them, and see the nickel-in-the-slot men, and take back all I had ever said about them, to arrange with the pimps that prostitution should be [word illegible].[15]

Rowell touched the highlights of developing Progressive ideology, that loosely grouped cluster of assumptions which much of Berkeley came to share by 1908. Included within this nucleus were the Progressive's concept of a "professional politician," and the desirability of injecting "non-partisanship" and "business principles" into the operation of municipal government. When Rowell spoke about the respectable vote while in Berkeley, those who listened shared equivalent meanings with him. They had no doubts as to who the respectables were, and where the line of exclusion was drawn by the nature of things. Berkeley reformers ardently agreed with Rowell that it was the moral responsibility of the respectables to take an active part in local government in order to elevate it to the level of decency.

In Berkeley among the articulators of these shared assumptions, as might be understandable, were professors of the University of California. On the occasion of the laying of the cornerstone of Berkeley's Town Hall, President Wheeler spoke out against the office seeker. The public welfare was, after all, too important to let local government be the sport of politics.

If we leave the management of our affairs to men who want to get office or emolument for themselves or their friends, or to men who have set themselves apart to the special work of running politics, then have we accepted oligarchy . . . . [16]

Professor William Carey Jones, the single leading spirit in the revision of Berkeley's charter -- the charter which had provided a seat for Schmidt -- denounced "boss rule and corruption" in American cities. Ward politicians were "those men who had deserted trade or trade had deserted them."[17] His lament for the city was fully shared by Thomas R. Bacon of the history department.[18]

Beverly L. Hodghead, a corporation lawyer and officer in San Francisco's Commonwealth Club, assisted Jones in constructing Berkeley's 1909 Charter. He took pride in the belief that adoption of that charter would result in the election of business men to office, and would screen out politicians.[19] His own election as mayor, shortly thereafter, must have convinced him of the wisdom of his own design. Echoing his mentor, Professor Jones, Hodghead stated, "The Politician is a man whose living is earned for him."[20] A man then who devoted himself to politics was in essence unworthy. His only skill is in the "art of getting office" and unlike the worthy business man, the politician "is only concerned about his profits."[21]

Only when Berkeley Progressives spoke with moderation did they refer to their self-defined enemy as a "politician," and what he managed as an "organization." At warmer moments the politician became a "boss," and the organization used to achieve individual and group objectives became a "machine." Both were dirty words in Berkeley argot. Both connoted sinister, corrupting influence.

General Interest Politics

In attempting to deal with the problems of health, sanitation, morality, and education, the solutions proposed by those who traveled in the club-church-university orbit were firmly resisted, and at times rejected, by West Berkeley. The Westsiders either did not share similar values, or else viewed the issues from a different vantage point. They definitely possessed a different set of priorities. The reform activists generally interpreted this set of circumstances within the context of general interest vs. special interest politics. West Berkeley men tended, more than others, to live and work in their own neighborhood which was both residential and industrial. If they had their way, their saloon would also be close at hand. Their ward representative on the town trustees identified more closely with his own neighborhood than any of his six colleagues. The press, in fact, never linked the others to their respective wards. Seventh Ward mothers preferred small, ungraded neighborhood schools rather than more distant, modern plants where education, according to those professionals who were believed to know, could be dispensed more effectively and for the lasting improvement of the child. The prime interests of the citizens of West Berkeley were with their section.

This outlook was interpreted as narrow self-interest by reform inclined Berkeley which prided itself for being above faction, party, and interest in the promotion of abstract and objective good. Fewer and larger schools, bonds for garbage, and bonds for rats were objective goods designed to advance the general interest of all Berkeley. Rarely did it occur to this sector of the Berkeley community that its personal or self-interest was more general in nature than that of West Berkeley, and that by riding the general interest hobbyhorse, it could have both its own interest plus a comforting sense of a higher civic morality.

In Berkeley in 1908 conflict over general vs. special interest politics coalesced around the ward system of representation in town government. Through the process of writing a new town charter, the reformers were able to eliminate political subdivisions and replace them with at-large representation.

Those in Berkeley who agitated for this form of representation were not willing to leave to fate or caprice the filling of such posts once the institutional tinkering had been completed to their satisfaction. Long before the decade of the 1920's, when the size of one's mahagony desk symbolized innate worth and value to society, the business-man's mystic existed. As early as 1904 President Wheeler exhorted "those who sit in the places of trust and responsibility for the management of institutions and of business affairs" to actively concern themselves with the political management of the community. For these gentlemen to shrink from such contact meant nothing less than "the commit-ment of political affairs to the hands of ignorance and corruption." For Wheeler, "good citizenship and large-minded, farseeing business-likeness" went hand in hand.[22] He returned to this same theme when called upon to speak on a civic occasion in 1908. "The business of managing a modern city is a plain practical matter . . . . It demands good business sense and strict attention; it is a big business enterprise."[23]

Also addicted to the business analogy, and with better reason because of his own personal involvement in corporate activities, was Beverly Hodghead. In his judgement (and as a co-author of the 1909 Berkeley Charter his judgement counted) the best way to govern a city was to give a free hand to a few "capable business men." They could then govern the town the way a board of directors manages the corporation.

> If the councilmen are elected solely because of their business
> qualifications if they represent the choice of the business intelligence
> of the community, they should be permitted to discharge their duty in
> respect to appointment to officers without regard to claims of political
> support.[24]

The only restriction upon the desirability of having the businessman in politics was that he too might violate the Progressive's concept of general interest politics. But here the danger seemed restricted only to big corporate types.[25]

The Berkeley club-church-campus-booster mind pictured business and professional men as representative not of their respective sectors of community or national life, but rather representative of a monolithic America. In order to inform William Carey Jones as to the qualities of the Los Angeles City Club, Professor Carl C. Plehn, economist and organizer of the Leagues of Justice and of the Republic, maintained that the mem-bers were "thoroughly representative business and professional men." They were a

73

"body of men of weight" and represented no "faction" or "special business interest."[26] President Wheeler agreed with him and added, besides being thoroughly representative, these businessmen were also "the best people,"[27] certainly a remarkable combination.

Unless Berkeley Progressives shared a set of equivalent meanings, they could not have conducted their political activities without a gigantic amount of internal confusion of misunderstandings. Much was implied by the continual use of such key terms as "the right people," "genuine men,"[28] "the right sort of men,"[29] the "best people in the world,"[30] "disinterested men,"[31] and "perfectly straight, high-minded"[32] individuals. The meaning seemed clear. These men were obviously those who stood for the good in political life. In other words, "our kind." Someone on the other side, therefore, became "a great sinister, corrupting influence."[33] Within this Berkeley circle there was general agreement on the dictates of "the cause of righteousness."[34]

Reform Berkeley Views San Francisco Graft

The year 1908 was historically significant for Berkeley. The town was on the eve of Progressive insurgency which was to capture the state and make a prosecutor of graft in San Francisco, governor of California. Bound up with this general Progressive reform spirit were Berkeley efforts to abandon its old governing charter in favor of the newly popular commission form of municipal government. Two items: graft prosecution in San Francisco and charter writing, consumed much Berkeley energy throughout the year. And very much at the center of these phenomena was the University of California.

Berkeley's Protestant churches were indeed concerned with governmental corruption across the bay in that center of ethnic and cultural diversity, San Francisco. Along with the preachers, the most articulate denouncers of San Francisco political life were those who were in close association with the University of California. President Wheeler, himself, invaded the citadel of sin on Sunday morning, June 7th, and from the pulpit of the First Unitarian Church of San Francisco preached on "civic conditions existing in this city." His text was taken from Jeremiah, "And I will make a new covenant with the house of Israel and of Judah."[35] San Francisco was to repent and make its peace with the Lord.

Graft prosecution in San Francisco appeared simple enough for Berkeley reformers. San Francisco supervisors had already confessed accepting bribes. The prosecution, officially under the direction of the District Attorney, was attempting to convict Mayor Eugene Schmitz and Abraham Ruef, his political adviser or boss, of extortion. The prosecution also tried to convict corporate officials of bribe-giving. The prosecution was actually being lavishly financed by the private capital of Rudolph Spreckels, a local millionaire, and was led by a special prosecutor on leave from the federal government. He was Francis J. Heney. The keen intelligence of the accused and of the defense staffs frustrated the desires of the prosecutors and with them, those in Berkeley who identified with the prosecution. As time dragged on Heney became less considerate of propriety, if not of basic personal rights, and all the time publicly branding the accused as guilty for the daily press.[36]

With Schmitz being half German and half Irish, and a Catholic besides, with Ruef being Jewish, and both stalwarts of the newly formed Union Labor party, it is understandable that San Francisco's ethnics and unionists were not the loudest of those crying for conviction. Also, at least half of the supervisors were Irish. As the prosecution proceeded to look into the sources of the bribe money, Nob Hill became less interested in proceeding with the investigations. As time passed, effervescent San Franciscans in general came to believe the prosecution a bore.

This was precisely what the Berkeley of the improvement club, the churches, and especially the campus could not understand and would not allow. Here was a clear case of righteousness making no headway against clear cut evil. In order that those dreaded, sinister influences not triumph over genuine men, mobilization took place for the avowed purpose of changing the direction of popular opinion regarding the graft prosecution. Under a letter dated February 12, about 150 persons associated with the University signed their names indicating their support of the graft prosecution and advocated more of the same.[37]

Two major rallies were held at Harmon gymnasium during which enthusiastic participants cheered pro-prosecution oratory. Heney himself appeared first. Introduced by Professor George Boke, organizer of pro-prosecution interest groups, Heney rose to speak amid wild and sustained applause. While his talk rambled, one major thrust rebutted anti-prosecution newspapers. He did not single out Yorke's Leader, but generally branded anti-presecution weeklies as "cheap" and criminal.[38]

By the time two distinguished Californians shared this same University platform six months later, public support of the prosecution in San Francisco had shriveled even more. If one judged from the University reception given to Rudolph Spreckels this fact would never be known, though. Spreckels, the financier of the prosecution, defended his special prosecutor in terms Progressives appreciated. He awarded Heney honorary membership with the best people, in spite of his background, because Heney was on the side of righteousness. Heney made mistakes but only while "acting in good faith" and besides, you shouldn't "get your mind off of the real criminal."[39] Presumably due process and legal safeguards were not equally applicable to those labeled "real criminals" by the best people.

The most dramatic and emotional profession of faith came from a prominent attorney and Progressive leader then on a temporary hiatus between appointments as Regent of the University of California. As an attorney Charles S. Wheeler recognized the tradition of providing counsel to all defendants. He even cited John Adams and his defense of a British officer. But the San Francisco graft case was different. Wheeler considered it a prostitution of an otherwise admirable principle. San Francisco defense attorneys were but hirelings chosen by grafters to impede the course of true justice. According to Wheeler, conditions in San Francisco had sunk so low that "one was almost afraid to whisper his love of country, his love of justice, upon California and Montgomery [Streets] . . . ." To him boss Ruef was "a self-confessed criminal and boodler and scoundrel, the wretch of a thousand crimes . . . ." From this premise, somehow the students of the University, thought Wheeler, had a choice presented them. They had to choose simply between "right and wrong." Fortunately Wheeler knew which way California would choose because he believed in "the womanhood of American women and . . . the manhood of American men." Somehow that made the decision clear and simple. Besides that, if California coeds did not know that bribery was a crime, then "you are unworthy to hold American male babes to your breasts (applause.)" Whether this clarified the issue any further is indeed doubtful. Nonetheless, Wheeler announced that from that night on he would march in the ranks with Heney and the prosecution, "I stand for law and order."[40]

Berkeley Reforms Itself

Professor William Carey Jones, the Berkeley spark plug of municipal charter revisions, possessed more than an academic interest in the political affairs of San Francisco. During the summer of 1907, he served as a consultant to the San Francisco Chamber of Commerce. The Chamber wished the advice of an expert concerning charter amendments then under consideration in San Francisco. While holidaying at Carmel by the Sea, he advised the Chamber that the proposed amendments seemed properly drafted, but that they were "conservative and modest." His personal recommendation was that more far-ranging changes would be necessary for the "political and moral rehabilitation of the city."[41]

While still in Carmel, Jones learned of what might have been interpreted as a first step toward this moral rejuvenation. Dr. Edward R. Taylor, Dean of Hastings College of the Law, an affiliate of the University of California, had accepted the post of Mayor of San Francisco. His appointment was dictated by the prosecution which extra-legally ruled the city. By then Mayor Schmitz had been removed from office following his local conviction and sentencing, a conviction later voided by higher courts. The confessed supervisors were kept in office by the prosecution and hoping for immunity, did the bidding of the prosecutors. Jones seemed unconcerned with the questionable democratic procedures involved in the installation of Taylor as mayor. More important than the means was the end. San Francisco was at last "redeemed."[42]

Jones' colleague, Professor George Boke, accelerated his own anti-graft activity by requesting monthly pledges to fund his League of Justice. His efforts were directed at countering the growing public apathy into which San Franciscans were sinking regarding the prosecutions.[43] In the League's official organ, the Liberator, he penned anti-graft editorials which, in the opinion of a Progressive leader and prominent San Francisco attorney, overkilled and did not provide sufficiently for the legal safeguards of the accused. Professor Boke's interesting response to the concern of his attorney friend and sympathetic colleague was that in his editorials he had earlier stated, and it was understood, that what he wrote held, "if . . . guilt shall be proven."[44]

Berkeley's attempts to reform San Francisco into its own image and likeness failed dismally. In time Mayor Schmitz's conviction was overturned and the political boss, Abe Ruef, was freed from jail. Even the supervisors found themselves in the odd position of having confessed to accepting money which no one wished to admit having offered. Driven beyond the point of tolerance (which admittedly was quite low) by the spectre of urban wickedness and corruption, Berkeley turned inward and reformed itself. Like the New Englanders of old who wished to be an example of true religion to the rest of the world, Berkeley wished to be an example of the best type of municipal government.[45] The fact that Berkeley hardly needed reforming seemed to matter little, least of all to Professor Jones who directed Berkeley's charter reform movement.

Jones was well prepared for his 1908 task of writing a new Berkeley charter. He had served on the Berkeley Board of Trustees and on the Board of Education, and seems to have aspired to the University presidency when the Regents turned East and chose Wheeler.[46] As a consultant to California municipalities, the professor seemed ever foraging for new ideas for perfecting the commission type government and ways by which the completed charters might be engineered into effect.[47] He was an eclectic who collected and studied the early commission forms and then advised California communities. He brought this type of expertise to bear on the creation of the Berkeley Charter finally effected in 1909.[48]

His basic plan provided for the popular election of a mayor and four councilmen. Each of the five would have one vote on the council and one councilman would head each of four city departments. All then would sit to vote policy and each councilman would supervise the execution of that policy which would pertain to his department. Included within his charter were the Progressive reforms of the initiative, referendum and recall. Critical to the plan was that elections were to take place on an at-large basis. The ward system of representation had to go.

The procedure involved in breathing life into the professor's creation was quite simple, given the relatively homogeneous nature of the Berkeley community. The town trustees authorized a freeholder election through which the voters were to select fifteen individuals who were to write the new charter. One slate of fifteen was put up by the Conference Committee of the Berkeley Improvement Clubs. It included, in addition to Jones, President Wheeler, and J. W. Flinn, the University Printer.[49] The others were prominent in club-church circles, not a few of whom would end up holding political office under the charter of their creation.

Visible opposition to this ticket emanated from West Berkeley which felt its interests were not sufficiently represented. The Citizens and Taxpayers League of West Berkeley created its own ticket which included twelve of the same individuals put up by the other improvement clubs. Jones remained but Wheeler was scratched as "merely a temporary fixture in Berkeley who might sever his residence at any time."[50] West Berkeley types were put up in place of those scratched, but to no avail. At the polls the Conference Committee's candidates won without the support of the Seventh Ward.

After one false start which required the process to be repeated, Jones' charter, as approved by the fifteen freeholders, became the basis for government in Berkeley following approval by Berkeley voters and the state legislature. One consideration seems quite relevant here. Of all the reasons given by Berkeley club-church-campus types for political action, the favorite and most often repeated was the need to return politics to "the people," and to remove the intervening "boss" from the body politic.

Trustee William Schmidt of the Westside's Seventh Ward opposed charter revision.[51] The candidates of the West were defeated in their bid for a place among the fifteen free-holders.[52] The final charter was approved by the Berkeley citizens over the opposition of the Seventh Ward. The net result was the legal termination of the Seventh Ward as a political entity and the removal of William Schmidt as a political figure. The Seventh Ward had opposed prohibition, opposed bonds for schools, bonds for garbage, and bonds for rats. Professor Jones' charter left the Seventh Ward not only without the political power of representation, it also left these people without a Seventh Ward. Perhaps they were not quite the people the church-club-campus types had in mind when they spoke of returning political power to the people. This, of course, was consistent with the re-form argot. If evil ran wild in San Francisco, at least in Berkeley the general interest had triumphed over special interest.

[1] Benjamin I. Wheeler to Theodore Roosevelt, Berkeley, July 7, Sept. 1, 1905; Wheeler to Nathan Moran, July 20, 1909, Wheeler MSS AUC: Edward L. Parsons to Chester Rowell, Berkeley, June 27, July 26, 1917, Rowell MSS, Bancroft Library, Berkeley; Daily Californian, April 1, 1908; Berkeley Daily Gazette, Feb. 5, 10, 12, 19, 20; Mar. 18; Aug. 15, 1908.

[2] E. F. Barry, Beautiful Berkeley (Berkeley: Youngs and Barry, 1904), p. 17.

[3] Berkeley Daily Gazette, Feb. 28; Mar. 30; April 10, 17, 21; May 1, 7, 13, 16, 25; Dec. 5, 1908.

[4] Wheeler to L. H. Wilson, Berkeley, Feb. 12, 1911, Wheeler MSS AUC.

[5] Berkeley Daily Gazette, March 5, 1908.

[6] Ibid., April 16, 18, 21; May 19, 1908.

[7] The story of the Progressive Movement in the State of California as seen from the vantage point of the movement's leadership is recorded in George E. Mowry, The California Progressives (Chicago: Quadrangle, 1963). For a view of the movement's mass support see Michael Rogin, "Progressivism and the California Electorate," The Journal of American History, IV (Sept., 1968), 297-314.

[8] Included within this group were the following: Berkeley Chamber of Commerce, Berkeley Charter Club, Berkeley Tennis Club, California Anti-Race Track League, Citizen's League of Justice, Conference Committee of Improvement Clubs, Fifty-Second Assembly District Republican Club, League of the Republic, North Adeline Improvement Club, Peralta Improvement Club, South Berkeley Improvement Club, West Berkeley Citizens and Taxpayers, West Berkeley Protective and Improvement Club, and the Women's Christian Temperance Union.

[9] Berkeley Daily Gazette, Feb. 13, 1908.

[10] Edward L. Parsons to Chester Rowell, Berkeley, Feb. 5, 1908, Rowell MSS, Bancroft Library, Berkeley.

[11] Joseph S. Brusher, S.J., "Peter C. Yorke and the A.P.A. in San Francisco," The Catholic Historical Review, XXXVII (July, 1951), 144.

[12] Walton Bean, Boss Ruef's San Francisco: The Story of The Union Labor Party, Big Business, and The Graft Prosecution (Berkeley: University of California, 1952), pp. 259-60.

[13] Berkeley Daily Gazette, July 6, 1908.

[14]Ibid., June 16, 1908.

[15]Chester Rowell to his father, Fresno, May 13, 1901, Rowell MSS, Bancroft Library, Berkeley. The world of communications before widespread use of the type-writer had advantages as well as limitations. While illegibility was a problem in this letter, script also provided a bonus. When writing about the Catholic priest delivering "his votes" Rowell started to write "the," as in "the Catholic vote," but crossed it out. These votes became then the personal property of a priest, possibly to barter off for advantage rather than merely an inert bloc. Rowell made the distinction between the Catholic priest's votes, which he sandwiched between brothels and gamblers, and the "respectable vote." That his respectables had shared experiences which led them to vote in bloc seemed never to have been considered.

To latter twentieth century Californians "nickle-in-the-slot men" may need ex-planation. Rowell would explain them as purveyors of pornography. By dropping five cents into the machine and turning the handle a series of pictures would flip past the viewer simulating motion.

[16]Monroe E. Deutsch, ed., The Abundant Life (Berkeley: University of Cali-fornia, 1943), p.307.

[17]Berkeley Daily Gazette, Feb. 22, 1908.

[18]Ibid., Jan. 21, 1908.

[19]Beverly L. Hodghead, "The General Features of the Berkeley Charter," a speech delivered to the League of California Municipalities, Sept. 21, 1909, p. 1, Doe Library, University of California, Berkeley.

[20]Ibid., p.7.

[21]Ibid., p. 1.

[22]Deutsch, op.cit., pp. 300, 302-3.

[23]Ibid., p. 305.

[24]Hodghead, op.cit., pp. 7,4.

[25]Wheeler to Theodore Roosevelt, Berkeley, Feb. 10, 1908, Wheeler MSS AUC.

[26]Carl C. Plehn to William Carey Jones, Berkeley, Jan. 22, 1908, Jones MSS, Bancroft Library, Berkeley.

[27]Wheeler to Jones, Berkeley, Jan. 20, 1908, Jones MSS, Bancroft Library, Berkeley.

[28] Chester Rowell to Friend Richardson, Fresno, Nov. 14, 1907, Rowell MSS, Bancroft Library, Berkeley.

[29] Wheeler to G. F. Peabody, Berkeley, Oct. 15, 1904, Wheeler MSS AUC.

[30] Wheeler to J. M. Taylor, Berkeley, March 6, 1907, Wheeler MSS AUC.

[31] Hodghead, op. cit., p. 9.

[32] Wheeler to Theodore Roosevelt, Berkeley, Aug. 20, 1907, Wheeler MSS AUC.

[33] Wheeler to R. Garrett, Berkeley, Nov. 8, 1905, Wheeler MSS AUC.

[34] Wheeler to N. M. Butler, Berkeley, Oct. 29, 1900, Wheeler MSS AUC.

[35] Berkeley Daily Gazette, June 8, 1908.

[36] Bean, op. cit., pp. 68, 261, 294.

[37] Ibid., p. 291; Call, March 2, 1908. A check of names listed in the press indicates that all were not faculty members at that time. Many would appear to have been graduate assistants.

[38] Berkeley Daily Gazette, March 13, 1908; Daily Californian, March 13, 1908. The University newspaper on March 12, 1908, incorrectly referred to Heney as "one of the University's most distinguished graduates . . . ." After a difficult childhood and irregular preparatory education, Heney obtained admission to the University at great personal sacrifice. Within the year, however, he was expelled for fighting. Bean, op. cit., p. 70.

[39] Berkeley Daily Gazette, Nov. 20, 1908.

[40] Loc. cit.

[41] C. H. Bentley to Carl C. Plehn, San Francisco, June 22, 1907; Plehn to William Carey Jones, Berkeley, June 24, 1907; Jones to Plehn, Carmel, June 28, 1907; Jones to C. W. Burks, Carmel, Aug. 5, 1907; Jones to Bentley, Carmel, July 20, 1907, Jones MSS, Bancroft Library, Berkeley.

[42] Jones to E. R. Taylor, Carmel, July 19, 1907, Jones MSS, Bancroft Library, Berkeley.

[43] George H. Boke to James D. Phelan, San Francisco, July 18, 1908, Phelan MSS, Bancroft Library, Berkeley.

[44] Boke to William Denman, San Francisco, Jan. 29, 1909, Denman MSS, Ban-

croft Library, Berkeley.

[45] Arthur Harris, City Manager Government in Berkeley No. Sp. 18. (Chicago: Public Administration Service, 1940), p. 5.

[46] "Searching for a President," undated and unsigned manuscript, William Carey Jones MSS, Bancroft Library, Berkeley.

[47] See C-B 536, Part III, Box 4, William Carey Jones MSS, Bancroft Library, Berkeley.

[48] Berkeley Daily Gazette, April 14, 1908.

[49] Daily Californian, March 26, 1908.

[50] Berkeley Daily Gazette, Mar. 2, 1908.

[51] Ibid., April 1, Oct. 7, 1908.

[52] Ibid., April 13, 1908.

CHAPTER VI

REGENT YORKE'S SUBCULTURE ON THE EVE OF PROGRESSIVISM

An Anti-Progressive Source

Even the most cursory examination of the Irish-Catholic-labor subculture, which idolized Father Yorke, demonstrates quite forcefully that it did not share equivalent meanings with the church-club-campus element of Berkeley. More than just a lovely body of water separated the minds of these two dissimilar subcultures. Berkeley very definitely was within the camp of the California Progressives, as has already been demonstrated. Yorke and his followers initially opposed that political movement.[1] In the "Preface" to his volume, The California Progressives, George E. Mowry regretted his subsequent lack of references to the papers of "the status quo in California," and men "who supported the rule of the Southern Pacific Railroad who were opposed to the democratization of state government." Mowry believed that such men either did not keep their papers or else were unwilling to allow scholars access to them. Had such papers been available, he acknowledged only that his narration "might have been modified here and there."[2]

That such records were not used seems more unfortunate than the author was then inclined to believe. Yorke's subculture was at first anti-Progressive. It voted against Hiram Johnson, the progressive Republican candidate for governor in 1910, and Yorke opposed Johnson's reforms once he had been elected. That Yorke and Catholic-labor in San Francisco first opposed the Progressives is correct. To conclude from this that as anti-Progressives they defended the status quo, however, is not altogether accurate. They advocated most forcefully the cause of unionism. This behavior was not in defense of the status quo, but was an innovating force in society, granted not one without local precedent. Progressives like the Berkeley middle class generally opposed labor unionism out of fear of being crushed between big labor and big business. Therefore, on the question of union labor, Yorke's anti-Progressives seemed more on the side of innovation, while the Progressives tended toward status quo or reaction.

Secondly, San Francisco's Irish-Catholic-labor, while not at all hostile to the Southern Pacific, tended to be more indifferent toward the railroad. Unlike the agricultural sector of the state, urban labor had fewer frustrating experiences of a first hand nature with the company. City workers had no produce to get to market via a monopolistic transportation system. The Southern Pacific simply was not very high on the subculture's list of concerns.

Also, while Mowry concerned himself with state rather than municipal government, to unequivocally place the Progressives on the side of democracy and, by contrast, to characterize the anti-Progressives as undemocratic is to place the stress on Progressive argot rather than behavior.[3] This is more easily done by not considering the anti-Progressives of which Yorke's urban subculture was a vital part. In fact the synthesis compiled from the records and memories of California Progressives does not at all present the views nor explain the behavior of a sizable urban sector symbolized by Yorke.

If Mowry's statement that anti-Progressives either kept no papers or else kept them private were applied to Yorke, it would be at best less than half right. Yorke and those with whom he associated and identified were closely bound together geographically. They were parish or neighborhood men with practical interests of a more limited scope. These men were in close contact with one another. When Yorke planned labor strategy with union officials, such sessions took place in his rectory parlor. Minutes, reports, and personal correspondence were seldom thought to be necessary. When a Berkeley professional wished to tell Chester Rowell that he liked his banquet speech, he had to write to him in Fresno. Rowell would file the original and the carbon of his response, with both ending up in the Bancroft Library at the University of California, the institution with which he felt such a bond. When a carpenter liked one of Yorke's anti-Progressive speeches, he wasn't much on writing so he would just tell Yorke the next time they met at the union hall, on the street car, or on the parish steps after Sunday Mass.

All anti-Progressives, however, were not inarticulate, illiterate, or secretive. Housed in the same building as the Rowell papers is what every author dreads -- an unexplored source. It is Father Yorke's weekly Leader, published in San Francisco throughout the period during which Progressivism flourished. Through it and through Yorke's surviving papers[4] and published works there emerges a view of passing events not shared by Berkeley and not explored by Mowry. For those Progressives caught up in their good versus evil syndrome and their addiction to the general interest concept of politics this is understandable.

Special Interest Politics

General interest politics, as opposed to special interest, assumes the existence of a consensus and as such, it is not capable of dealing with innovation which is beyond that consensus. Innovators, those who are beyond the consensus and who are trying to create a new consensus which will include themselves, are viewed by those sharing the general interest concept of political life as self-seekers who oppose the common good. In this role the hill dwellers cast West Berkeley. In this role, too, fitted Irish-Catholic-labor in San Francisco, at least for those who believed in the general interest concept of reality. This group did not include Yorke. He rejected the campus-club-church consensus which dominated Berkeley.

In constructing a conceptual framework for the history of Irish-Catholic-labor in the United States, the most profitable approach has been the plotting of the interaction between the cultural baggage brought from Ireland and the American realities through time and changing circumstances. The vast bulk of scholarship and other writings dealing with this American subculture has concerned itself almost exclusively with the urban industrial centers of the North East. Because of the greater concentration of Irish-Catholic-labor in that section and because of the treatment it has received, the subcultural history of the Eastern urban Irish has been virtually accepted as a national synthesis. When variety is injected into the resulting popular image, it is too often reduced to the perceived differences between New York and Boston.

In New York the political machine was the focal point with individuals finding place, direction, and fulfillment within the Tammany organization. Under Irish leadership the machine was characterized, among other things, by stability, predictability, and endurance. As in their Catholic Church, structure and hierarchy prevailed with power being dispersed, but unevenly so. Lesser functionaries within the machine were politicized men who attended to their tasks firm in the knowledge that with persistence and time they too would advance. Generally they believed the formal government of the city to be illegitimate and only their informal one, the organization, truly to represent the people.[5]

The Boston chapter of this subculture, while sharing some attributes with their New York cousins, generally has not profited by the comparison. The New Yorkers seem more sophisticated and certainly more adept at formal organization. For Boston's Irish, the tribal chieftain stood in place of the machine and for many of his forty years of prominence, James Curley led the clan -- alone. Not trusting subordinates, he preferred to lead from a position of solitude drawing his sustenance from the undifferentiated mass. When a humble New Yorker wanted a push cart license, he went to his precinct captain first, not to Charles Murphy, the Tammany boss. In Boston he had to begin at the top because there was no hierarchy. Curley maintained his place and obtained elective office because his personal behavior pattern appealed to his constituents, but he was unable to transfer support to others and in the end had nothing to pass on to a successor.[6]

San Francisco has had no enduring Irish machine, no clan chieftain the likes of Curley. The reason for this varient stems not from their cultural heritage, but rather from the varieties within the American reality. The San Francisco Irish needed no invisible government to protect them from an enemy establishment. Unlike New York, San Francisco was still young when the Irish arrived. Society remained rather open and fluid, and the Irish joined in the early scramble with others for places of preferment. Unlike the Boston Irish, those in the West were not overawed by cultural superiority. In the early days they could compete with New England transplants while displaying examples of their own remarkable entrepreneurial optimism.

Opportunities for work and satisfaction of rising expectations existed to the extent that Irish-Catholic-labor never fell under the control of a local demagogue for any extended period. (If Yorke be classified as a demagogue, his Roman collar prevented his seeking office). By 1900 San Francisco was a distant but attractive haven for members of this immigrant group. While most made the Eastern centers their permanent home, a few merely paused to replenish their resources and move on. Some did it within a lifetime while others lingered a generation or more. In either case San Francisco was their far western choice. Rather than being an industrial complex, the city was a commercial center of great diversity, increasingly sophisticated and cosmopolitan. In addition, a large and growing Catholic population called it home.[7] In San Francisco conditions for growth and success favored them. No other ethnic bloc was so large or well situated so as to control city affairs -- least of all those who considered themselves one hundred percent American. Likewise they never approached an absolute majority and so had to find their way through cooperation rather than through the raw force of numbers.[8]

As a virile, acquisitive minority, San Francisco's organized labor was beyond Berkeley's mental consensus. The Irish, who were highly influential within the union movement and who dominated the local Catholic Church, were in an awkward position vis-a-vis this dominant Berkeley mind. As a highly politicized minority, the Irish have generally followed the principle in America that political problems should be solved through the harmonizing of conflicting views. When interests collide, the Irishman in politics would be inclined to push for the most generally acceptable solution, the one with the broadest support, the one by which fewer people would be alienated, even though it was not their personal proposal.[9] In short, as a highly politicized minority of marginal men, operating at times as a line of skirmishers in advance of the main body of immigrant America, Irishmen fitted easily into the role of interest brokers. As the children of immigrants or as immigrants themselves, they understood the wants and needs of other lower class Americans. As English speakers who had learned the practical realities of Anglo-Saxon based laws, from the short end, and who seemed intrigued by the intricacies of urban power, they were well suited to this role.

In the mind of church-club-campus Berkeley such brokerage among interests was not as the Irish immigrant saw it: logical, workable, and democratic. Instead it was the epitome of special interests fighting among themselves for illicit preference within the body politic in blatant disregard for the general interest. Those involved in such brokerage were beyond the circle of "genuine men." When Berkeley rejected this traditional role of the Irish immigrant, which by contrast was quite conservative and minimal, one only wonders what was their candid reaction to Yorke.

The Anti-Reform Impulse

Father Yorke held in utter contempt those who considered themselves the reformers of the day. Politics to him was mostly a question of men. Some politicians were the best of men, others the worst. The political context or system did not determine individual behavior. It was rather the man that made politics what it was.[10] The "holier than thou" reformers, in Yorke's opinion, could give lessons to the most hardened ward heelers.

They are fighting not on any great principle but reform and good government. The reformers are hardly in before they have to be rereformed . . . . The whole thing seems to be an endless chain of turn the rascals out until it would take the apparatus and memory of a train dispatcher to know who is in jail and where and who are on the road.[11]

As for the proposed remedies espoused by the reformers -- get a new charter, a new party, a new candidate or get the people into politics and remove the bosses -- Yorke considered them all claptrap.[12] The stereotyping may seem extreme, but Yorke actually approved of politicians giving turkeys to the impoverished at Thanksgiving as a means of maximizing their vote on election day.[13]

The issue over which Yorke and his subculture so strongly disagreed with the dominant sector in Berkeley was the San Francisco graft prosecution which followed the great earthquake and fire of 1906.[14] In addition to serving as a model for political, social, cultural and possibly religious conflict, the graft prosecution demonstrates the degree to which those with whom Yorke identified had permeated the political vitals of San Francisco. All this was in marked contrast to the Berkeley scene.

The classic stereotype of the relation of the urban politician to graft was succintly formulated by that true practitioner of the art, George Washington Plunkitt, the sage of Tammany Hall. Once holding four public offices simultaneously and being paid for three, he knew his subject. Plunkitt seems to have been the originator of the fine distinction between "clean" or "honest graft" as he preferred to call it, and "dirty" graft.[15] To use your inside knowledge of municipal construction plans in order to realize a real estate profit was an example of honest graft. According to Plunkitt, there was always so much honest graft lying around, only the dullard tempted the penal code.

The City and County of San Francisco in 1906 had seventeen dullards on the eighteen member Board of Supervisors.[16] They not only took dirty graft but also admitted it. All were Union Labor party members. Nine of the seventeen were identifiable Irish. Innocents in politics, their slate had been swept into office during a freak election. Despite their common party label, they were not organization men. They were loners pulled together by boss Abe Ruef at the last moment in order that his Union Labor Party could enter a ticket. Ruef's purpose in selecting them was to maximize the vote behind his candidate for mayor. When the entire slate was elected in 1905, he was as surprised as anyone and none too happy. Since the supervisors were not political men, disciplined by a life of machine tending, Ruef's control over them immediately broke down and in the end he admitted it. Uninhibited by the restraining influence of a continuing organization, they were free to, as Ruef put it, "eat the paint off a house."[17]

Contrary to what reformers might conclude, in actuality there existed in San Francisco no institutionalized political machine to which these supervisors or anyone else owed loyalty. Unlike their counterparts in the East, these men owed fidelity and obedience to no political entity beyond themselves. In a sense the Berkeley reformers did not comprehend, they truly were independent of party and faction and were responsive, unfortunately, to themselves alone. Whether or not these men were "representative," or "genuine," they assuredly were independent!

Ruef's Union Labor Party was new and temporary and their relations with it had been only cursory. In the East, a ward man advanced to Alderman only after he had proven his talent, ability, and orthodoxy through years of loyal party service. Unlike this, the San Francisco supervisors considered themselves free agents and behaved accordingly. In this sense then, boss Ruef was no boss at all. Although the Union Labor party was elected under his guidance, it was not a continuing, pervasive machine, controlled by a hierarchy with Ruef as the apex.

The San Francisco graft prosecution was instigated by a few prominent private citizens which included Rudolph Spreckels, Fremont Older who edited the San Francisco Bulletin, and ex-Mayor James Phelan who was Irish, Catholic, but not labor. The avowed targets were not particularly the lowly supervisors, but rather the higher-ups who were presumed to include Mayor Eugene E. Schmitz, Ruef, and bribe-giving corporate executives.

Mayor Schmitz had many political assets in pluralistic San Francisco. He was a union man in a union town, wearing in fact the Union Labor party label. His greatest advantage in the city of his birth, however, was his own religious and mixed ethnic background. Being German and Irish he claimed affinity of blood with forty-six percent of San Franciscans. Of all who attended church, Schmitz sat with the massive Catholic majority (eighty percent). Being personally attractive, with grooming, he was able to mingle at ease with the city's elite and blended well at the Cliff House speaker's table when President Theodore Roosevelt was banqueted in 1903.[18] Irish-Catholic-labor could identify with him, and, at least vicariously, could share in his social lionizing.

Prosecuting Schmitz was his negative (or positive depending on one's politics and self-identity), Francis J. Heney. In his case his father was Irish and his mother German. His religion, as we shall see, was in doubt. Assisting Heney in the close stalking of the prey was another Celt, William J. Burns. This cunning sleuth already possessed a fine reputation with the secret service and later was to organize his famous private detective agency.

The long series of graft trials were held for the most part before Superior Court Judge Frank H. Dunne. And between him and Schmitz flared enduring enmity, enhanced by Dunne's denial of the mayor's request for a change of venue. Dunne, of course, was Irish also.

Other Irishmen cast in supporting roles included Matthew I. Sullivan and Joseph J. Dwyer. On behalf of the district attorney's office, they assisted the new prosecutor, Hiram Johnson, after Heney was shot in court. In the Ruef camp, on the other side of the aisle was Frank J. Murphy, himself prosecuted later on the charge of attempting to bribe a juror through a third party. Murphy's acquittal followed the court appearance of Father H. H. Wyman of Old St. Mary's who testified as a character witness. The case against Murphy had depended on the testimony of a felon, the convicted intermediary.

The final case in the prosecution was almost an all-Irish (defined broadly) finale. Patrick Calhoun, grandson of John C. Calhoun and president of the favor-seeking United Railroads trolley company, was defended against bribe charges by the team of Moore, Moore, and Barrett. During the trial this trio served five days in jail for contempt for protesting the political behavior of their fellow Gael, Judge William P. Lawlor.

Reasonably enough Irish-Catholic-labor did not warm to the prosecution even though it was, on close examination, not a strict case of a political machine of theirs being exposed by Protestant respectables. The respective sides were not clearly drawn into opposites across all three variables. Labor was on the side of those being prosecuted. Catholics were on both sides, but detracting from the weight of Phelan's orthodoxy was the questionable nature of Heney's and Dunne's fidelity to Holy Mother the Church. And besides, Phelan himself, mingled with the rich and had used the police against labor while mayor. As for the location of the Irish, those with the prosecution were explained away in behavioral terms. They became traitors on their own, despised like the infamous informers of the old country who betrayed their own blood for preference from the alien enemy.

Yorke Views San Francisco "Graft"

From the start Yorke's followers considered "the graft" (the term he consistently used when writing about the prosecution) as an attempt of a few rich men to deprive the people of their rightful possession -- political power democratically acquired. They objected to the district attorney's office, bankrolled by private capital and supported by a crusading newspaper, the Bulletin, seizing political power in a not so bloodless coup. All but one member of the Board of Supervisors had confessed to accepting bribes and hoped for immunity from the prosecution. While in this precarious position the Board, at the mercy of the district attorney's office, did its bidding. Once Mayor Schmitz was deposed the prosecution dectated his interim replacement. The prosecution forced the Board to appoint one of its own discredited members. All this transpired while Heney and Spreckels sought, along with the District Attorney, a more suitable successor whom they later would install permanently.[19]

The prosecution, which drew its sustenance in San Francisco from a private and narrowly based source, next had the Board of Supervisors appoint Dr. Edward R. Taylor as mayor. The interim appointee dutifully stepped aside. The ultimate in respectability, Taylor had served the community both as a physician and as an attorney. He had as its president, directed Cooper Medical College and at the age of 68 was Dean of Hastings College of the Law, a University of California affiliate. Taylor, the prosecution that installed him, and the Bulletin that supported him were all odious to Yorke. His discontent increased when Taylor was elected in his own right in November 1907.

When the prosecution felt it had dispatched the ethnics it turned on the bribe-giving corporate executives. This was a strategic error of the first magnitude. Irish-labor-politicians in league with Nob Hill finance-capital then forged a new coalition and recaptured City Hall in 1909 behind Irish-born Patrick McCarthy. The day McCarthy stood for election, the Irish-controlled Building Trades Council declared a holiday throughout San Francisco's construction industry. Labor turned out and not trusting the prosecution's government, they spent $2,500 on poll watchers.[20] When their man won by a large margin they considered political power to have been returned to its legitimate possessors through traditional democratic means. Their democratic counter-stroke had ousted the prosecuting junta and they were pleased.

Throughout the period of the graft prosecution, Yorke's interpretation of the entire episode was consistently pro-Schmitz and viciously anti-prosecution. He portrayed the entire prosecution as a "conspiracy between [sic] several rich men of San Francisco to obtain possession if the City and loot it."[21] Yorke identified Spreckels as the original conspirator who gradually drew others into his web. Yorke described him as "an uneducated, fat-witted, bigotted block of beefy conceit," who "could never aspire to anything higher than to drive a brewery wagon" except for his money.[22] What actuated Spreckels was the frustration of alleged plans to gain control of the city's street car system with the wealthy ex-Mayor and later Progressive United States Senator, James Phelan. As mayor, Phelan had outraged Yorke by using police to protect strikebreakers. Yorke lambasted Phelan in barnyard Gaelic[23] and dogged him so relentlessly through the rest of his political life that Phelan believed pure malice to be the only motivation.[24] Comparing him to a bubonic rat and labeling him a "congenital defective,"[25] Yorke, through innuendo, suggested that Phelan had used public money for other than public use after the disastrous 1906 fire. When the Board of Supervisors turned down their trolley requests, Spreckels turned on Mayor Schmitz and with business men created "a huge corruption fund" to be used to railroad Schmitz.[26]

At this point Spreckels allegedly broadened his conspiracy to gain control of the municipal government by bringing into camp the daily papers including Fremont Older's Bulletin (labeled the "Bullytin" by Yorke), District Attorney William Langdon, and chief prosecutor Heney. The abuse Yorke heaped on Phelan was exceeded only by his treatment of Heney whom he branded an "informer," an Irishman who sacrificed those of his own blood in return for preferment at enemy hands.[27] Heney's ill-repute in Yorke's eyes was compounded by his belief that Heney had allowed the San Francisco Irish to believe that he was a Catholic when he had been married by a preacher. Yorke even doubted Heney had ever been baptized. As for his chief investigator, William J. Burns, he was "a spy" and "must be the rankest kind of a four flusher."[28]

Yorke's dislike for Fremont Older antedated the prosecution at least to 1904. The Bulletin had run a story in which Yorke's brother appeared as a graft-accepting paving contractor. On that occasion Father Yorke lashed out at the Bulletin as a "festering cesspool" and at Older as a "dirty cad" below the moral level of a "yellow cur." He accused Older of deserting his child and the child's mother while he "rioted in Del Monico's with a cast-off trollop of the barracks."[29] By 1908 no evidence suggests Yorke changed his opinion.

Throughout the years of the prosecution's activities, Yorke remained mostly silent or guarded on Ruef and the supervisors. Any public defense would have been awkward at best considering their admissions of guilt. Yorke did, however, speak out ardently for Schmitz and against the prosecutors. He referred to Ruef only obliquely when he wished to link his admitted corruption to the University of California professors who were crying out for good government.[30] Ruef was a California honor graduate and also a graduate of Hastings College of the Law. But only at a church benefit up in Sparks, Nevada, did Yorke categorize Ruef as an informer along with Heney his prosecutor,[31] never did he do so in his metropolitan press. He never used vitriolic language on Ruef or the supervisors, and after the episode ended, his worst judgement of them was that they too were part of the conspiracy against Schmitz. Yorke's response to the obvious question of why, under those circumstances, men would brand themselves as criminals, was highly suggestive of his deep conviction concerning the character of Spreckels. If these men would, wrote Yorke, "swear they were bought by one millionaire, what would be wonderful in the fact that they were bought by another millionaire?"[32] Such remarks seemed directed more at the prosecution than at the supervisors and may have been posited by the needs of his conspiracy thesis.

Also included in Yorke's grand conspiracy thesis was Judge Dunne, referred to as a tool of injustice and a "wretched little renegade"[33] who "looks like the before-taking advertisement of a patent medicine."[34] What provoked Yorke to the point of rage was the fact that Dunne and the other judges who presided over various aspects of the graft trials had Irish names. And on one occasion he wondered, "Are we to believe that the descendants of all the Irish informers have broken into the California Bar?"[35] These men were damned in Yorke's eyes as apostates, quislings, and Uncle Toms all in one. In a biographical sketch, Yorke characterized Dunne as a native born son of Irish parents whose ignorance prevented him from making a living as a practicing attorney. Fortunately for him his brothers were in the saloon business, and through their political-fraternal connections succeeded in having young Frank elected to the bench. Yorke circulated the rumor that "to further his ambition . . .he foreswore his father's faith and joined the Masons." To add hypocrisy to his infamy in the eyes of Irish-Catholic-labor, Yorke told them the ignorant renegade's brother continually declared that he would quit the Masons after the next election.[36]

Of all those individuals identified with both sides of the graft prosecution, Yorke felt there was but one "decent person."[37] He was Mayor Eugene Schmitz, the conspiracy's victim. Schmitz, unlike the others, steadfastly maintained his innocence throughout the encounter and through later life. What was also important to Yorke was his thorough orthodoxy. He was a communicant of the Catholic Church and a Union Labor party member in good standing. Father Yorke was a leading advocate of the Union Labor party and gave Schmitz favorable publicity in his Leader from its inception.[38] In 1903, the Leader advertized Schmitz for mayor as a member of their own ethnic subculture and a man "beyond reproach."[39]

Yorke stuck with him through bad times as well as good, as few others did. Through the period of the trials Yorke was resolute. He was convinced that running down graft was not the intent of the prosecution. The prosecutors were engaging rather in political trials, whereby, they used the excuse of good government to oust the democratically elected labor government through undemocratic and extralegal means. Yorke was ever ready to point out the prosecution's disregard for individual rights of the accused and the lack of basic fair play for Schmitz in Dunne's court. And because of this personal treatment, Schmitz's guilt or innocence had not really been determined.[40]

Yorke himself maintained that Schmitz was innocent, while University of California based groups organized for the purpose of stimulating the prosecution to even more strenuous efforts. When the District Court of Appeals reversed the Schmitz extortion conviction, Yorke felt vindicated.[41] When the California Supreme Court upheld that decision, Yorke was in controlled ecstasy.[42] Even though the conviction had been set aside, Yorke felt the conspiracy had succeeded. For after Schmitz had been first convicted and sentenced, he was removed from office and, as has been seen, the prosecution then controlled the apparatus of city government.

Yorke's position on Schmitz is actually less enlightening than his view of the supervisors since Schmitz denied all wrong doing. Unlike Berkeley reformers, Yorke saw Schmitz simply as an innocent victim of a conspiracy of anti-labor millionaires seeking to control the city government by undemocratic and extralegal means. While not mentioning the supervisors as such, Yorke's treatment of their behavior is very revealing. Yorke questioned the limited definition of graft used by the prosecution and shared by the dominant culture which, like the Berkeley Progressives, tended to be native, middle and upper class Anglo-Saxon, and Protestant. In his breezy manner he asked what he thought to be a fundamental question, "What is graft?"

> When a Catholic gives a dollar to a priest to have a Mass said for him the Protestant shouts "graft." When the Protestant gives his minister a fee for funeral services the atheist shouts "graft." When Heney gets $42,000 from a corporation for 42 hours' work, all his enemies shout "graft." When Ruef gets $100,000 from another corporation also for work the whole town yells "graft." But the still, small voice still asks the question, "What is graft?"[43]

Unlike the Tammany boss, George Washington Plunkitt, Yorke did not divide graft into honest versus dishonest graft where one's wits determined which to take.[44] Yorke's categories were "gentlemanly graft" as opposed to the graft of laboring people.[45] But like Plunkitt and unlike general interest Berkeley, Yorke was convinced everybody got his share or tried to when he had the chance. The only difference was that some graft was illegal and other graft was not. For Yorke the problem existed as much within our legal institutions and cultural mores as within the local body politic. Both sides were pursued only their self-interest. One side was able to use the judicial apparatus on the other. Gentlemanly graft was honest while the graft taken by the labor supervisors was dishonest. Yet, everyone got his graft! Everyone who knew the Spreckels family, wrote Yorke, "knew the clan were not in this anti-graft business for their health."[46] Yorke noted that the United States Senate had passed a subsidy bill for Pacific ships even though, in his opinion, their service was unequal to that of the ships in the Atlantic. To this Yorke tied the Spreckels family.

> In other words, Congress wishes to make the Spreckels [family] a present of a big sum of public money for doing less work on this side of the continent than is required on the other.

> It is not graft. The Lord forefend! It is merely the result of legitimate enterprise. How impudent of these poor laboring people to try to bread into the preserves of the gentry! They got a few measly cents, and should be put to jail. The gentlemen get their millions and demand a seat in the Senate.[47]

Yorke Views Berkeley Reformers

How different Yorke's interpretation of the graft prosecution was from those who cheered Spreckels and Charles S. Wheeler in Harmon gymnasium on the Berkeley campus. Spreckels and Wheeler saw themselves standing up for a higher morality along with patriotism and the womanhood of the American woman. They saw themselves as promoters of the common good. Yorke saw them as grafters all, the only difference being in the level of graft they pursued, and possibly their degree of hypocrisy. Interestingly enough, both sides saw themselves standing for law and order. When the State Supreme Court upheld the reversal of Schmitz's conviction Yorke hailed it as "the greatest victory for law and order, for justice and Americanism" in recent times. Through "the long debauch" of the prosecution, he "never despaired of the republic and the inborn justice of an American community."[48]

Though the prosecution was ultimately frustrated in its attempt to place Schmitz behind bars, he was nonetheless removed from office. The law school dean installed in his place was, in Regent Yorke's opinion, undoubtedly one of those "good-government incompetents."[49] Midway through ex-Dean Taylor's full term as mayor, Yorke objected to his all but complete elimination of Catholic municipal appointees.[50] When Irish-Catholic-labor's Patrick McCarthy took City Hall at the next election, Yorke bade farewell to "the experimenter, the good government fakir, the reform crook and the hairy poet . . ." and looked forward to "a period of sanity" in political life.[51] Real people as opposed to genuine men were back in power again.

The respective stances of Yorke and the Berkeley reformers relative to the San Francisco graft prosecution were symptomatic of their deeply held convictions concerning the Progressive reforms of the day. Yorke objected to reformers and their reforms. He particularly resented "the ardent advocates of 'Good Government'" who lived in suburbia while trying to reform the city.[52] On one such list of twenty-three he included five Berkeleyites and a University Regent residing in Marin County just north of San Francisco.[53] Toward the end of his own career Yorke reflected on the career of Chester Rowell, the Progressive leader so respected by the Berkeley reformers. By then Rowell, himself, was a Regent of the University of California. In retrospect Yorke considered Rowell to have been "a parasite all his life on the American body politic, and like all such parasites, has come to consider himself a being of finer clay . . . . He is simply a petulant charlatan, a hidebound hypoc[r]ite."[54]

Yorke opposed the entire gamut of Progressive reforms -- the initiative, referendum, recall, women's suffrage, and public regulation of utilities -- and voted against them when he had the chance.[55] He was definitely not among those who would experiment with government and was convinced that the philosophical underpinnings of Catholicism, not experimentation, held the solutions to modern problems.[56] Certainly for Yorke, the development of new knowledge at most was to be clearly subordinated to reconsideration of the known. Within the initiative, referendum, and recall, Yorke foresaw the real danger of organized minority interests such as have come to plague some liberal school board members in conservative areas. This insight was available to Yorke and not to Progressives, such as those in Berkeley, because he viewed these persons, the instigators of such direct government, as an organized minority while they considered themselves as the people at large.

Yorke's opposition to the initiative and referendum stemmed from his belief that legislation was a complicated affair which needed experts, by which he meant regular politicians. To relieve lawmakers of this task was to fragment responsibility in such a way that it ceased to exist. The politician, like the doctor and the lawyer, had his legitimate specialized calling.[57] Yorke rejected the prevalent assumption that the politician was a roadblock between the people and the government. Rather it was only through the professional expertise of the regular politician that the democratic process functioned.

Yorke's animosity for Berkeley rose to an all time high in 1908. An underlying cause for this feeling, without a doubt, was a sense of alienation ranging over the religious, cultural, social, economic, and political differences which separated those with whom Yorke identified from the composite identity emanating from reform Berkeley. This alienation existed in 1900 when Yorke attacked the University of California and its Board of Regents. After closer contact with Berkeley for five years as a Regent, the flame of hostility again flared up. This time it was caused by Berkeley's ardent support of the graft prosecution which Yorke considered a grossly unfair attack on his own people and the democratic process, by their enemies and by renegades. West Berkeley was fine. Yorke empathized with that section of the town. "West Berkeley was inhabited by people, but East Berkeley by college professors."[58] "College Town Berkeley, New Charter Berkeley, Berkeley of the Bungalows, the Gargoyles and the Hillside Club." This was the Berkeley Yorke considered "the most unnatural town on the continent . . . ."[59] In well cultivated sarcasm he referred to those who dominated the upper contour lines as "the hill tribes," "mountaineers," and "the better 'clawses.'"[60] When Professor George H. Boke, organizer of the anti-graft leagues, criticized the California appellate court's reversal of the Schmitz conviction, Yorke branded him crude morally and absurd philosophically. He then added, "If Professor Boke be a specimen of the lawyers turned out at Berkeley, we don't wonder at the phenomenon of Abe Ruef."[61]

At this same time Yorke interpreted the behavior of President Wheeler as making the University of California a side show to the Progressives, which included "that flatulent Pharissee, Chester H. Rowell." He characterized their political organization, the Lincoln-Roosevelt League, as "an alliance of Republican soreheads with the San Francisco graft." (When Yorke said "graft" he meant what Progressives called the 'prosecution.") And when all these allies protested their civic virtue, they were merely squealing like "the little hogs that the big and strong hogs have forced away from the feeding trough." In the last analysis, Yorke considered the political behavior of President Benjamin I. Wheeler "not only to be silly, but to be positively dangerous."[62]

Yorke flatly rejected the basic assumptions so cherished by the Berkeley reform element. He resented the professors in general for their distrust of what he saw as popular government. To him their new charter reform efforts represented little more than an attempt to limit the popular element in government. It was "their means of warfare on the denizens of the flat." Writing for those with whom he identified he stated, "We do not believe that college professors are fit to make or administer political

94

institutions." In flat rejection of the sentiment prevailing in Berkeley, Yorke proclaimed his firm belief that "political institutions can be administered only by politicians."[63]

From 1900 to 1908, Father Yorke became more familiar with persons and events in Berkeley. With greater knowledge, however, came greater revulsion. His sub-cultural predispositions, plus a rather unique personality, placed him in a position not in harmony with the dominant elements in Berkeley, elements which, of course possessed their own predispositions and personality.

[1]Michael Rogin, "Progressivism and the California Electorate," The Journal of American History, IV (Sept., 1968), 301-2.

[2]George E. Mowry, The California Progressives (Chicago: Quadrangle, 1963), pp. v.-vi.

[3]Samuel P. Hays, "The Politics of Reform in Municipal Government in the Progressive Era," Pacific Northwest Quarterly, 55 (Oct., 1964), 160-9.

[4]The Yorke collection is located in the archives of the University of San Francisco in the Richard A. Gleeson Library, San Francisco.

[5]Daniel P. Moynihan, "When the Irish Ran New York," The Reporter, 24 (June 8, 1961), 32-4.

[6]William V. Shannon, The American Irish (rev. ed.; New York: Macmillan, 1966), p. 211.

[7]Religious Bodies, 1916, United States Department of Commerce, Bureau of the Census, pt. I (Washington: 1919), pp. 243-4.

[8]Twelfth Census of the United States, 1900, United States Census Office (Washington: 1901), I; clxxvii, 439, 877.

[9]Edward M. Levine, The Irish and Irish Politicians: A Study of Cultural and Social Alienation (Notre Dame: University of Notre Dame, 1966), p. 169.

[10]Peter C. Yorke's Vallejo, California, speech Sept. 24, 1900, in unnumbered Composition Book, Yorke Collection AUSF.

[11]Yorke's Sparks, Nevada, speech Nov. 27, 1907, in unnumbered Composition Book, Yorke Collection AUSF.

[12]Yorke's Vallejo, California, speech Sept. 24, 1900; III, "Proposed Remedies" in same unnumbered Composition Book, Yorke Collection, AUSF.

[13]The Leader, Dec. 5, 1903.

[14]Walton Bean, Boss Ruef's San Francisco: The Story of The Union Labor Party, Big Business and The Graft Prosecution (Berkeley: University of California, 1952).

[15]William L. Riordon, ed., Plunkitt of Tammany Hall (New York: E. P. Dutton, 1963), pp. 3-6.

[16]The Board of Supervisors is the legislative body for the consolidated City and

County of San Francisco. In the first decade of this century the entire eighteen stood in the same election. All seats were filled at large, not by ward.

[17]Bean, op. cit., p. 215.

[18]A. Lincoln, "Roosevelt and Muir at Yosemite," Pacific Discovery, XVI (Jan.-Feb., 1963), ill., 18.

[19]Bean, op. cit., p. 229

[20]Robert E. L. Knight, Industrial Relations in the San Francisco Bay Area, 1900-1918 (Berkeley: University of California, 1960), p. 220.

[21]The Leader, March 14, 1908.

[22]Loc. cit.

[23]Ibid., March 28, 1908.

[24]James D. Phelan to Editor of the Irish World (New York), Feb. 29, 1924, Phelan MSS, Bancroft Library, Berkeley.

[25]The Leader, Feb. 15, 1908.

[26]Ibid., March 14, 1908.

[27]Yorke's unnumbered Composition Book marked "Vallejo, Sept. 24, 1900," even though later items are included, Yorke Collection, AUSF.

[28]The Leader, March 14, 1908.

[29]Ibid., Oct. 22, 1904.

[30]Ibid., Feb. 8, 1908.

[31]Yorke's unnumbered Composition Book marked "Vallejo, Sept. 24, 1900," Sparks, Nevada speech, Yorke Collection, AUSF.

[32]The Leader, Mar. 14, 1908.

[33]Ibid., Feb. 29, 1908.

[34]Ibid., April 4, 1908.

[35]Ibid., Feb. 29, 1908.

[36]Ibid., March 14, 1908.

[37] Yorke's unnumbered Composition Book marked "Vallejo, Sept. 24, 1900," Sparks, Nevada speech, Yorke collection AUSF.

[38] The Leader, Jan. 11, 1902.

[39] Ibid., Oct. 3, 1903.

[40] Yorke's unnumbered Composition Book marked "Vallejo, Sept. 24, 1900," Sparks, Nevada speech, Yorke Collection AUSF; The Leader, March 14, 1908.

[41] The Leader, Jan. 11, 1908.

[42] Ibid., March 14, 1908.

[43] Ibid., April 11, 1908.

[44] Riordon, op. cit., pp. 3-6.

[45] The Leader, March 28, 1908.

[46] Loc. cit.

[47] Loc. cit.

[48] Ibid., March 14, 1908.

[49] Ibid., Jan. 15, 1910.

[50] Ibid., Jan. 16, 1909.

[51] Ibid., Jan. 1, 1910.

[52] Ibid., Feb. 1, 1908/

[53] Loc. cit.

[54] Yorke's Scrapbook, vol. 2, p. 225, Yorke Collection AUSF.

[55] P. C. Yorke, Educational Lectures (San Francisco: Text Book Publishing, 1933), pp. 220-1, 241-3, 248-9.

[56] Ibid., p. 221.

[57] Ibid., pp. 244-5.

[58] The Leader, Aug. 8, 1908.

[59]Ibid., Jan. 23, 1909.

[60]Ibid., Aug. 8, 1908.

[61]Ibid., Feb. 8, 1908.

[62]_Loc. cit._

[63]Ibid., Aug. 8, 1908.

CHAPTER VII

FATHER YORKE IN THE ROLE OF REGENT

Yorke's Response to Appointment

The sitting of Father Peter C. Yorke with the Board of Regents of the University of California as one of its members is an example of a partisan leader who, through a direct assault, penetrated an institutional fortress which he had considered hostile to himself and those with whom he identified. His behavior, once he became a member of the inner circle, was rather interesting, very understandable, but also quite unexpected, given his temperament and previous pattern of responses. And in addition it was in ways quite disappointing. He was pleased with the honor bestowed upon him by his friend, Governor Henry T. Gage, during the midnight of his administration. Yorke accepted the post as a symbol through which his subculture was to have its share in the administration of the University. He felt Irish-Catholic-labor was entitled to a representative on the Board because of its force of numbers. Through Yorke this "sector of the tax-payers" had demanded representation, and through the demand obtained its rights.[1]

Whatever deep inner satisfactions Yorke may have enjoyed because of this appointment, he never displayed them publicly. In fact, if his readers missed four issues of The Leader in early 1903, they would not have known of Yorke's appointment from him. And even if they did receive those issues, only by very careful examination would they detect references to the latest honor bestowed upon their champion. Yorke was very restrained in the public enjoyment and display of this new title, Regent. After February of 1903, reference to his Regency was not mentioned in his newspaper. This was true through his entire term which ended in 1912.

With the position also came residual honors, such as the invitation to luncheon with the President of the United States, Theodore Roosevelt, following the latter's commencement speech at Berkeley in 1903.[2] Never did Yorke allow his subculture the opportunity even to entertain the thought that he had passed over and become one with those whom he had vilified in 1900 before the St. Mary's College graduates. On February 14, 1903, a very brief news article stated the fact of Yorke's appointment being confirmed by the California State Senate with but little anti-labor opposition.[3] That notice seems to have been Yorke's last reference to his position as a Regent.

Yorke was outwardly cool toward his appointment from the start, and always cautious. He displayed a pattern of behavior shared by many of his fellow Irish, one which may have been ingrained through generations of struggle and disappointment. Yorke did not count the office of Regent as his until after the Senate had acted upon Gage's appointment. Up to that time he preferred to keep his impending appointment quiet, and wait for the accomplished fact. Above all he refused to act on the assumption that he was a Regent out of concern that through some unforeseen intervention he would be denied the appointment. If such did transpire, what points might enemies be able to score then? He did not expose himself, instead he proceeded with the type of caution born of countless frustrations and last minute disappointments which were part of his heritage.[4]

President's Response to a New Regent

Following the Governor's announcement of Yorke's appointment, President Wheeler initiated a series of responses which formed a pattern consistent with his role within the institutional structure. He tried, first through personal overtures, to bring Yorke to a more friendly disposition toward himself and therefore toward the University. And this may have been difficult for a man of Wheeler's temperament. Certainly he had not forgotten the St. Mary's blast. Just recently Yorke had added to this by calling him an uninteresting speaker and "a gentle and pious head of a Sunday school . . . ."[5] He also objected to Wheeler's periodic pulpiteering.

Yorke of course objected to the ease with which Protestant ministers glided between the classroom and their meeting houses. For him being a priest meant forever, and he seemed to resent that this was not so for ministers also, or in Wheeler's case, ministers' sons. He looked upon the comparative ease with which ministers gave up or switched callings as a lack of commitment. And by gravitating toward the open arms of institutions of higher education, he undoubtedly felt they were obtaining soft berths at public expense. This he objected to as part of the public which had not been consulted. While Wheeler had never been a man of the cloth, Yorke still alluded to him when he vaguely wrote, "We know one or two [University Presidents] who long ago renounced the pulpit with all its works and pomps, but yet these gentlemen stray back once in a while."[6]

Wheeler took no official note of these slighting remarks, and even acted a bit prematurely by inviting the Regent-designate to a University meeting and a luncheon with members of the state legislature, those who were to act on his pending appointment.[7] Immediately after confirmation by the Senate, Wheeler made a second overture to Yorke by inviting him to address the faculty and students of the University at one of their regular meetings.[8] Yorke accepted this offer with pleasure and seems to have genuinely enjoyed his subsequent campus exposure.[9]

Through the remainder of the year Yorke was the recipient of personal invitations to social events at the University, and also to dramatic productions.[10] Beside these tokesn of Wheeler's desire that Yorke feel included within the University camp, he also expended his time promoting undertakings in which Yorke was vitally interested. He spoke at a St. Patrick's day banquet in 1903, at which he out-Irished the Irish in his praises for their Gaelic language, and chastized them for not studying and cultivating it with greater diligence. In his editorial response Yorke wrapped his own cause of Gaelic revival in the cloak of Berkeley scholarship so conveniently provided by the President of a University whose "influence . . . is growing every day."[11] Here Yorke approved of what Wheeler said and also approved of his saying it. He hoped that this "student of the Irish" would be an inspiration to the Irish themselves. [12]

While no documents survive to indicate Yorke was responsible for Wheeler's Irish night appearance, no other Irishman was better situated to arrange for such a speaker. He had ample opportunity, less than two weeks before, when he shared a Berkeley platform with the President and then dined with him shortly after as Wheeler's guest. Wheeler wished, of course, to maximize University support among all possible constituencies. If Yorke would have invited him, he probably would have spoken from Yorke's pulpit too. Needless to say, Wheeler never faced such a decision.

Wheeler did however move into fringe areas, which as an outsider and observer of Yorke's subculture, he presumed Yorke should have been interested int. The Berkeley Newman Club was one. In fact Wheeler seemed to take a greater interest in its activities than did Yorke. He attended receptions and introduced guest speakers. [13] When Yorke assisted at the dedication of the Ridge Road building, no mention of his Regency was made in The Leader. [14] On that soil Yorke's Archbishop was in charge, not the University. The sermon of the day was delivered not by orator Yorke, but rather by Father Charles A. Ramm who, as the University's honor graduate of 1884, and as a quiet diocesan organization man, was acceptable to both cultures. As a convert to Catholicism out of Berkeley he became the marginal man, but from the reverse direction, with the appropriate advantages and limitations. As such, he succeeded to Yorke's seat as Regent in 1912.

By 1905 Wheeler was still displaying outward manifestations of consideration toward Yorke, tapping his expertise for a translation of a popular Gaelic drinking song, and forwarding him extra copies of publications on Irish topics. These items were not attended to be Wheeler personally but by secretarial assistants. [15] The reduction of Yorke on the President's order of priorities by then was consistent with the priest's attendance record at Regent's meetings. By 1905 his attendance was sporadic, with extended absences which were to become even longer as the years passed. Yorke's second and last address to the faculty and students of the University of California was delivered in January of 1906. At that time Yorke was receptive to Wheeler, but saw less and less of him due to his own declining attendance at Board meetings. He did attend the January meeting, and the following day Wheeler followed up their conversation concerning the campus speech. [16] During the preceding calendar year Yorke attended four of the fourteen meetings of the Regents of the University of California.

An Uneasy Relationship

As had already been noted Yorke publicly denounced Wheeler as a "positively dangerous" man during the heated graft controversy of 1908. [17] This total disagreement with Wheeler, and the greater Berkeley consensus which he symbolized in so many ways, was a difference which was essentially political and cultural rather than educational. Yorke repelled by Berkeley's commitment to political Progressivism and by Wheeler who embraced it so fondly.

On educational matters, the area in which Wheeler and Yorke officially met, some difference of opinion existed, but these were not frequent and they always remained within the normal, structured dynamics of institutional decision making. Once the President and Regents applied themselves to the day to day problems of the University, Irish Catholicism simply was not a meaningful guide for those confronted with the need for this kind of decision making. Compiling budgets, lobbying with the legislature, investing endowment, recruiting of professors, and bronzing radiators had no Catholic/non-Catholic secret formula. After denouncing Wheeler publicly as that "positively dangerous" man, Yorke stood with the other members of the Board, and approved a resolution commending President Wheeler for having elevated the University to a new position of prestige among institutions of higher learning. In the educational sphere Yorke, after six years on the inside, cast his vote of confidence for Wheeler and the type of education pursued at Berkeley.[18] Yorke abominated the political climate of Berkeley which he and his subculture found so alien. Yet within the major educational enterprize at Berkeley his subcultural predisposition did not serve as a unique guide for action once he had accepted the legitimacy of the entire undertaking.

Also, Yorke seemed able to compartmentalize the different parts of his life. As a partisan editor he rejected the suggestion that Berkeley graduates were better fitted for political offices than other individuals, who include his fellow ethnic aspirants. He reacted against any hint of what he considered a politically privileged class, writing, "It would be a monstrous thing if Berkeley were to be the breeding cage of an aristocracy."[19] As a new Regent of the University, standing before the assembled faculty and students in Harmon Gymnasium, he seems, on might judge, to have had a different perspective. Looking at the students around him he said that the University was more than just a place for research and teaching. It was a place where the children of California might be "fitted to carry out every trust." Apparently reversing himself, he exalted, "You are to my mind the picked ones of the State. You are sent here for service. You are the conscripts of a noble warfare." Before he turned to leave, Yorke reminded his young listeners, "You have advantages that are given to few, you are in the van of all the peoples, and the heirs of the ages."[20]

Granted, Yorke was a man of strong emotions who could warm to the responses of a crowd, whether physically present in front of him or more distant as subscribers to his paper. As far as President Wheeler was concerned, however, Yorke was not a disruptive factor within the University community. Being both energetic and prudent, Wheeler's efforts to defang California's first militant ethnic minority critic of the University took more substantial form than simply exposing him to the campus community, and granting him social access to persons of prominence beyond Berkeley.

"Irish Studies" at Berkeley
Only one innovation took place within the University during the Yorke years as a Regent which directly concerned him. This was the establishment of instruction in Gaelic, the language so warmly regarded by Yorke. This innovation did not come about through deliberations within the faculty, but rather was effected from the top down. Prior consultation on the matter did take place between Wheeler and Yorke but surviving

evidence suggests that Wheeler, rather than Yorke, initiated a proposed professorship of Irish.[21] Wheeler suggested that for "some representative Irishman" to provide such a professorship would be an act well received by the University.[22]

Yorke responded to the half overture, half request, by recognizing what interested him and conveniently ignoring what did not. Yorke undoubtedly felt he did not become a Regent to serve as a convenient intermediary through which the University could draw even greater financial support out of his Irish community, a community which Yorke felt was already paying double for education. To qualify Irish children for proper citizenship in this world and the next, Yorke felt Catholic schools were necessary even at Catholic expense, while through general taxation they also supported public education which often went unpatronized by them.[23] Yorke agreed with Wheeler that the teaching of Celtic at Berkeley was desirable, and it would improve the image of the University among his subculture, which then was not favorably disposed to the institution. While Yorke remained strategically vague as to how such instruction might be financed, he not only met Wheeler's suggestion of a professorship, he went beyond it. Yorke spoke in terms of an established chair of Celtic Languages and Philology.[24]

By the fall the two had reached a modus vivendi. Just prior to adjournment of the monthly Board meeting, on September 8, 1903, Yorke offered a resolution that a Department of Celtic languages and Philology be established. This department was to be staffed by one individual at the academic rank of instructor with a salary of $1,000 per year. Wheeler expressed himself in favor of the resolution, which then carried and was referred to the Finance Committee.[25]

A premature, critical response within the Catholic community quickly appeared in the Institute Journal, a publication which Yorke read. Objecting to the emolument attached to the post, fear was voiced that only a "broken down hack . . . cast out of other positions" would take the post. Any man of quality, it was argued, would devote his main efforts to other activities, and merely his spare time to Berkeley. In short then, Gaelic at California was merely "political sop . . . to the vanity of the Celt."[26]

Whether a sop or not Yorke seized and used it for all it was worth, and even more. Four days after action by the Regents, Yorke's Leader, published an account without referring to Yorke's own role. This account distorted the actual events in such a way that what appeared seemed a much greater concession to Yorke and his followers than actually was the case. Three statements were not correct. Contrary to what Yorke published for Irish-Catholic-labor, no "Gaelic Chair" was established, it was not to be occupied by a "Professor of Gaelic" and no "immediate steps" were planned "to make the study of Gaelic one of the most important branches of the curriculum of the State University."[27] Yorke was present at Board meetings when discussion took place and when the decisions were made.[28] He was conversant with the very significant difference which academic types place on the official title "professor," as opposed to "instructor." During his earlier warfare with the Catholic University of America he displayed a firm grasp of what an endowed chair was. Here then the imprecise grasp of terms by the Irish-Catholic-labor subculture allowed the appearance of a much greater concession by the University than in reality took place. Yorke rather than using this occasion to exercise an educative function, encouraged confusion. His readers were misled.

After approval by the Board, the next question to be faced by Wheeler was the actual staffing of the newly created position. Yorke himself, while quite competent in the field, was not a candidate by virtue of his position as a Regent. The self-imposed rules under which the Regents operated prevented any of their number from accepting a position of profit within the University. But if Yorke himself were unavailable, the next best was a facsimile of the same. One name had been in circulation since the Gaelic question came up originally. It was that of Father Richard Henebry, the Catholic priest who had been brought from Ireland to the Catholic University of America to occupy their endowed Gaelic chair. He was a native speaker who had been sent by the University to Germany where he received the Ph.D. He had been supported by Yorke in his unsuccessful tenure battle with the Catholic University. By 1903 he had returned to County Waterford, Ireland, where he was an active cleric.[29] Except for his earlier academic embroilment, Henebry must have appeared an ideal candidate from the vantage point of a keeper of institutions. His appointment to the faculty as an instructor in Gaelic would please Irish Catholicism and Yorke. The only critical factor missing was his nonmembership in the local Union Labor party; but given his past political behavior, Henebry could be expected to manage such matters for himself.

At first Wheeler was unfamiliar with the man's academic qualifications and in the interests of Berkeley academic standards felt that any candidate for the Gaelic position ought to be well prepared in the "comparative philology of his discipline; at least understand the scientific bearings of his subject and the comparative philology of the Celtic dialects."[30]

Hearing this, Yorke reassured Wheeler that Father Henebry was his man. He described him as an Aryan philologist who knew "Sanskrit and the Teutonic range." He was the first native Irish speaker with a Ph.D. in his discipline.[31] Not only, then would Henebry be politically acceptable to local Irish-Catholic-labor and personally acceptable to Yorke, his formal academic qualifications were equal or superior to those staffing the University's departments. He seemed a rather unique candidate who qualified by everyone's standards. Yorke served as an intermediary between Wheeler and Henebry so that by the end of the year all Wheeler had to do was make the official offer.[32] Henbry accepted and the following spring, Wheeler placed his appointment before the Board. They approved his one year appointment as an instructor in Celtic Philology, effective July 1, 1904.[33]

This appointment seemed too good to be true. Meeting or exceeding all criteria for the position, Henebry tested no man's principles. Yorke started preparing Henebry's way in the spring of 1904 by editorializing on Celtic at the University summer session. He encouraged attendance among teachers particularly, but also for those seeking degrees along with the general public.[34] The May budget compiled by the Regents contained, for the first time, the inclusion of a Department of Celtic staffed by Richard Henebry, instructor in Celtic Philology. His salary was to be $1,000.[35]

Twice Yorke championed Henebry's academic career. Once, as a popular outsider, he used his newspaper and his influence within Hibernian organizations, to try to gain tenure for him at the Catholic University of America. Failing that, he inflicted what injury he could on the institution through public assaults on its faculty. Then as a member of the Regents of the University of California, he engineered an appointment at Berkeley, only to have it too fall short of fulfillment, and for the same reason, Henebry's health.[36] Though he never displayed it publicly, Yorke must have felt disappointed by his other self.

The following spring the Finance Committee decided the allotment for Celtic should be left in the budget even though no prospect existed on the horizon for its use.[37] Later Wheeler recommended and the Board accepted Henebry's resignation, effective October 3, 1905.[38] During the next years the unfilled position and the appropriations remained in the budget, the latter being raised to $1,200. In 1900-1910, Celtic was omitted entirely.[39]

The matter remained dormant before the Board while Wheeler pursued it at the administrative level. The Board's approval of the teaching of Celtic as a policy remained unchanged. They simply ceased carrying the unused appropriation on the yearly budgets. When Wheeler located a new candidate in 1910, he simply recommended to the Board that a special appropriation be voted at the old rate. In this case, however, the person he recommended would not draw the full salary. He was being brought to Berkeley from Hoboken, New Jersey, as a student, and in such a capacity Wheeler was authorized to pay him that portion of the salary he thought adequate as a scholarship for the lad. The The understanding was that he would "conduct some elementary instruction in Celtic."[40] The following fall Wheeler announced to the Board that Joseph J. O'Hegarty had been appointed to teach Irish at a rate of $500 per year. His academic title, if it is to be called such, was reader.[41] His status was in the undefined area between student and faculty, being junior in both. He entered Berkeley in 1910 in the freshman class.[42]

This new arrangement for Celtic at Berkeley was quite a retreat from Yorke's original efforts for a distinct Irish chair, and even from his agreement with Wheeler for an instructorship staffed by an Irish priest possessing both a Ph.D. in the field and a reputation for ethnic militancy. This second Celtic appointment took place at a time during which Yorke had absented himself from Board meetings. The calendar year during which O'Hegarty's scholarship and appointment were arranged coincided with a perfect record for nonattendance by Yorke. As in the Henebry case, however, he made the most out of an appointment which was much less than he had initially wished. Yorke announced to his subculture that courses in the Irish language were to be offered at Berkeley for credit in what he termed, incorrectly so, a "newly created department of Gaelic." Joseph O'Hegarty was invested with the honorary rank of professor, and the purpose of his course, as stated by Yorke, was to enable students to read classical Irish -- old and middle. O'Hegarty's approach was declared to be through the medium of modern spoken Irish,[43] a noble objective indeed for one without the academic preparation inherent in the acquisition of a university degree.

President Wheeler in all likelihood viewed the arrangement with O'Hegarty as an interim maneuver, for during O'Hegarty's first year of service, he engaged in negotiations for a regular faculty appointment in this area. Wheeler offered an associate professorship of French and Celtic Philology to J. T. Gerig who promptly declined the offer.[44] The University grew and developed during these years, and the effects were such that they contributed to greater specialization and compartmentalization of faculty, and clearer divisions between disciplines and departments. Wheeler had tried unsuccessfully to create a joint appointment in French and Celtic, a move which was contrary to the contemporary trend. He followed this up by an adjustment among his resident linguists. He transferred one, who had held an appointment in French and German, to the Department of Romance Languages where he became an associate professor of French.[45] Being unsuccessful in his attempt to graft French and Celtic in a single appointment, he advanced the former at the expense of the latter, allowing Celtic to remain in the young hands of O'Hegarty while at the same time raising his salary to $600 a year.[46]

During these years Wheeler felt no pressure from Regent Yorke who was displaying publicly his satisfaction with O'Hegarty. Yorke continued to refer to the reader as "Professor," and by the spring of 1912, had installed the honorary Prof in the non-existent Chair of Celtic.[47] He noted that student interest in Gaelic at Berkeley was increasing and attributed the increased enrollment to O'Hegarty, "the right man in the right place."[48] Certainly not unrelated to O'Hegarty's acceptability was his link with Yorke's community. On Friday nights he conducted Gaelic instruction in Yorke's parish hall for members of the Yorke Chapter of the Gaelic League, an international Irish organization devoted to the preservation and spread of Gaelic as a living language. Yorke advertized this instruction as providing individual attention to each class member, and following O'Hegarty's University of California methodology[49] -- whatever that might have been.

That Yorke should appeal to the authority and prestige of the University of California, and linguistic methodology pursued under its auspices, is less indicative of any conversion of Yorke's disposition toward the institution than it is of a strange anomaly within Irish-Catholic-labor. At the same time, members of the subculture were attracted and repelled by universities and the intellectual life. To have a son or daughter attend college was a mark of distinction, one in which parents could take pride. But if that son or daughter, through behavior or speech, went beyond the limits of orthodoxy, a ready made and acceptable explanation existed -- he learned it at college from those professors.

In O'Hegarty's case Yorke dealt with a person who though he lacked the academic preparation consistent with professorial rank, was at least as well prepared as those teaching elementary Gaelic in Ireland at the time. Yorke represented him as a professor, and was untroubled about his orthodoxy. Under such circumstances the negative side of the subculture's orientation to universities was subdued or absent so Yorke was able to draw upon the respect for learning. Here, maybe even unconsciously, Yorke momentarily used the University of California to help promote his life-long interest -- Gaelic revival.

Unfortunately Yorke did not succeed in the language revival movement; neither did the young reader he had blown into a professor succeed at Berkeley. He left the University without ever having received his degree, and remained an affiliate of the class of 1914, whereabouts unknown.[50]

Regent Yorke's Response to Duty

In the main, decisions made by the Regents during Yorke's years were not the type over which sophisticated and experienced men held sharply different opinions. Consensus rather than conflict was the order of the day. Most business before the Regents from 1900 to 1912 did not call for debate, alignment, and votes. Instead it was simply accepted on the recommendation of President Wheeler, the man who was the choice of the Regents for the administrative head of the University, the man in whom they placed confidence.

On the limited number of occasions when measures were voted upon, they were almost always passed by a unanimous vote, procedural matters being an exception. A meaningful analysis of Yorke's voting behavior is not possible since Yorke did not vote most of the time. This is so because most of the time he did not attend the monthly Regents' meetings. When he did attend, he normally voted in unanimity with the others. Yorke did not attend at all during the months between his appointment by the lame duck Governor and his approval by the State Senate. He attendance was regular through the creation of the Celtic post and the appointment of Henebry. Thereafter it became sporadic. As the years advanced, Yorke's periods of nonattendance lengthened, with 1908 as somewhat a dividing point. After the climax of the San Francisco graft prosecution, Yorke attended only three meetings in the remaining four years of his appointment. From November 9, 1909, he attended no meetings. Through his nine year tenure of office, the Regents of the University of California called one-hundred and twenty meetings of which Yorke participated in thirty-one. He attended only twenty-five percent of the meetings of the full Board.[51]

No evidence exists to indicate that Yorke ever gave any explanation for his chronic absenteeism. During these years his health was good. He was vigorous and active. When he left for a European trip he seems to have notified no one at the University. This behaivor was in contrast to that of other Regents whose business called them out of the state and abroad, or else was otherwise pressing. On such occasions they requested relief from demanding committee work, or they sought leaves of absence.[52]

The regular general meetings of the Board were held monthly in San Francisco, except for the ones preceding Commencements which were convened at the University. Before the San Francisco earthquake and fire the Regents met in the Hopkins Institute of Art which contained a room for their exclusive use.[53] Later the place was adjusted from time to time, but San Francisco remained the usual site. When Yorke attended his first meeting in 1903, a standard order of business had already been introduced which remained constant through the years. The calling of the roll was followed by consideration of the minutes, the President's report, and those of the standing and special committees. Other agents of the Board could then be heard, followed by old and new business. This order of business was formalized in the "Orders of the Board" in November 1904.[54]

The standard procedure was for Wheeler to be the initiator. On his motion routine matters would be approved by the full Board. Other items would be referred to the respective committees into which the Board was subdivided. There they would be considered and reported back to the full Board with a recommendation. The President of the University was an ex-officio member of all committees.[55] Each year a Committee on Committees was appointed by the chair to recommend membership for the standing committees. These recommendations by the ad hoc committee were always quickly approved by the Board, and after that, by the Governor. Through the first years of the century, there were about nine standing committees with some fluctuation not only in membership but also in the committees themselves.[56] The division of labor was such that most Regents served on one committee. A few served on more than one. Yorke's initial assignment was to the Lick Observatory Committee which was charged with responsibility for the University's Observatory located on Mount Hamilton, about fifty miles south of Berkeley.

Through the years Yorke was never placed on any other committee, neither was he ever appointed to an ad hoc committee. These facts, plus his attendance record at general meetings, might suggest his disinterest in the details of University affairs. After his initial flurry of activity, communications between this Regent and his University were reduced to little more than a one-way flow of arid announcements concerning meetings which Yorke never attended, and inquiries concerning his correct address and telephone number.[57]

Yorke's committee attendance record, during the period of 1903-1911, indicates he was not consumed by any interest in the advancement of science. Fragmentary records indicate him present at three out of twenty-seven meetings for a total of twelve percent.[58] Needless to say Yorke was never elected chairman or vice-chairman and, in fact, no evidence exists indicating that he ever visited the Lick Observatory, or took any interest whatsoever in its existence. These committee meetings which Yorke ignored, were informal gatherings in the San Francisco office of Regent Charles W. Slack. In addition to authorizing payment of the Observatory's bills, appointments and promotions were considered, salary adjustments were considered, and physical improvements in plant and equipment were voted and sent to the full Board. This committee passed also on expeditions to distant places such as Sumatra, Labrador, Spain and Assuan.[59]

During these years other Regents who served on the Lick committee at least obtained an administrative acquaintance with the world of science. This was obviously not true of Yorke. Here he was consistent with a central feature of the history of American Catholicism, significant disinterest in scholarship and science.[60] Unfortunately Yorke combined in himself not only this common American Catholic deficiency, but also a second deficiency, one not common among American Irish leaders. Yorke was not an organization type characterized by caution and reserve, nor was he oriented to the future. The result was that Yorke nurtured none of his University contacts, neither President Wheeler nor Dr. William W. Campbell, Director of the Lick Observatory and future President of the University.[61] The more typical mode of behavior within his sub-culture would have been to participate in the business of the University, which included committee assignments, and through attention to the assigned tasks, good will, and not a little good cheer, to first of all enjoy sharing in the manipulation of a large and powerful institution. Beyond this few political Irishmen in such circumstances could have resisted the opportunity for cultivating an expanded circle of well-placed persons.

As a Regent of the University of California, Yorke embodied the greatest deficiency inherent in American Catholicism and ignored a source of its strength.

[1]Daily Californian, Mar. 16, 1903; The Leader, Feb. 21, Mar. 28, 1903.

[2]Benjamin I. Wheeler to Peter C. Yorke, Berkeley, May 11, 1903, Yorke MSS AUC.

[3]The Leader, Feb. 14, 1903.

[4]Yorke to Wheeler, San Francisco, Jan. 15, 1903, Yorke MSS AUC.

[5]The Leader, April 26, 1902.

[6]Ibid., Dec. 13, 1902.

[7]Wheeler to Yorke, Berkeley, Jan. 14, 1903, Wheeler MSS AUC.

[8]Wheeler to Yorke, Berkeley, Feb. 28, 1903, Yorke MSS AUC.

[9]Yorke to Wheeler, Oakland, Mar. 4, 1903, Yorke MSS AUC; Daily Californian, March 16, 1903.

[10]Wheeler to Yorke, Berkeley, Mar. 19, 1903, Yorke MSS AUC; Yorke to Wheeler, Oakland, May 6, 1903, Wheeler MSS AUC; Yorke to Wheeler, Oakland, Aug. 29, 1903; Wheeler to Yorke, Berkeley, Sept. 22, 1903, Yorke MSS AUC.

[11]The Leader, Mar. 28, 1903.

[12]Loc cit.

[13]Daily Californian, Feb. 14, 1908, April 22, 1903.

[14]The Leader, Mar. 10, 1910.

[15]V. Henderson to Yorke, Berkeley, Feb. 27, 1905; to Yorke, Berkeley, June 26, 1905, Yorke MSS AUC.

[16]Wheeler to Yorke, Berkeley, Jan. 10, 1906, Yorke MSS AUC.

[17]The Leader, Feb. 8, 1908.

[18]UC Regent's Minute Book, XVI, 108.

[19]The Leader, April 4, 1903.

[20]Daily Californian, Mar. 16, 1903.

[21]Wheeler to Yorke, Berkeley, May 29, 1903, Yorke MSS AUC.

[22]Loc. cit.

[23]The Leader, May 16, July 25, 1908, Dec. 16, 1911.

[24]Yorke to Wheeler, Oakland, May 30, 1903, Yorke MSS AUC.

[25]UC Regent's Minute Book, XIV, 114.

[26]Institute Journal, XI (Oct., 1903), p. 7, in Yorke's "Patten Book," Yorke Collection, AUSF.

[27]The Leader, Nov. 14, 1903.

[28]UC Regent's Minute Book, XIV, 129-30.

[29]Yorke to Wheeler, Oakland, Nov. 12, 1903, Yorke MSS AUC.

[30]Wheeler to Yorke, Berkeley, May 29, 1903, Yorke MSS AUC.

[31]Yorke to Wheeler, Oakland, May 30, 1903, Yorke MSS AUC.

[32]Yorke to Wheeler, Oakland, Nov. 12, 1903, Yorke MSS AUC.

[33]UC Regent's Minute Book, XIV, 179.

[34]The Leader, April 9, 1904.

[35]UC Regent's Minute Book, XIV, 215, 219.

[36]V. Henderson to Yorke, Berkeley, July 14, 1904, Yorke MSS AUC.

[37]UC Regent's records of the Committee on Finance, VIII, April 20, 1905, located in the office of the Secretary of the Regents of the University of California, Berkeley, California.

[38]UC Regent's Minute Book, XV, 36, 479.

[39]Ibid., XV, 324, SVI, 18, 177.

[40]Ibid., XVI, 203.

[41]Ibid., XVI, 229.

[42]Robert Sibley, ed., The Golden Book of California (Berkeley: California Alumni Association, 1937), p. 580.

[43] The Leader, Aug. 27, 1910.

[44] UC Regent's Minute Book, SVI; 308, 318.

[45] Ibid., XVI, 319-20.

[46] Ibid., XVI, 302.

[47] The Leader, Feb. 3, 1912.

[48] Ibid., Feb. 3, Jan. 27, 1912.

[49] Ibid., June 22, 1912.

[50] Sibley, op.cit., p. 580.

[51] Statistics compiled from responses to roll calls recorded in UC Regent's Minute Books from Feb. 10, 1903, to Mar. 12, 1912.

[52] UC Regent's Minute Book XVI, 93, XV, 132, 162; XIV, 330.

[53] Ibid., XIV, 281.

[54] Ibid., XIV, 282.

[55] Loc. cit.

[56] Ibid., XIV, 50, 300-01, 358; XV, 103, 362-3; XVI, 93, 194, 325.

[57] See CU-1, Box 63, Yorke MSS AUC.

[58] See minutes of the Committee on Lick Observatory, Sept. 25, 1888, to -. S.15, B.18, Office of the Secretary of the Regents, University of California, Berkeley, California.

[59] Ibid., pp. 72-3, 58, 87.

[60] John Tracy Ellis, American Catholics and the Intellectual Life (Chicago: Heritage Foundation, 1956), p. 56.

[61] Sibley, op.cit., p. 173.

CHAPTER VIII

REGENT GARRET W. McENERNEY: A COMPARATIVE FIGURE

His Milieu and Yorke's

In stark contrast to Yorke's behavior as a Regent of the University of California was the response of another Catholic to his appointment to the Board. A historical figure contemporary to Yorke, he served as a Regent through the Yorke years. Yorke was familiar with him for he too was part of the same San Francisco subculture, only not at its nucleus as was Yorke. Garret W. McEnerney was a San Francisco attorney who served as the attorney for the Catholic Church in Archbishop Riordan's diocese.[1] In such a capacity and likely even before his appointment, McEnerney would have come to the attention of Father Yorke, since Yorke had served for a time in the Chancery office himself. In 1902 McEnerney traveled to The Hague with Riordan where he pursued the interests of the Church before The Hague Tribunal.[2] Yorke's random notebooks contain periodic press clippings relating to McEnerney's advancing legal career.

The common meeting point for these two men was the Catholic Church in San Francisco. Their next area of greatest commonality was the University of California. McEnerney's extraordinary length of service, forty-one years, stretched from his initial appointment in 1901 to his death in 1942. He was reappointed in 1904 and at sixteen year intervals thereafter.

Both of these Regents were part of the Irish-Catholic subculture of San Francisco, but to varying degrees. Yorke was the leading figure towards which many were attracted and from which some, including his Archbishop, were repelled. McEnerney possessed no public followings nor did he identify with the unionists. He was born in California of Irish descent. McEnerney was fond of his Irishness while his professional status liberated him from the usual social and economic confines of a working class subculture. Throughout his life he maintained an interest in things Irish and during his lengthy Regency promoted Irish culture within the University of California.[3] He did not participate in the usual ethnic clubs and societies which flourished within the avid Irish-Catholic-labor subculture of San Francisco.

Though an unassuming gentleman, McEnerney definitely was not a low brow, and his brand of Irish was not Yorke's.[4] Also, the respective personalities of these two Regents were divergent. While Yorke, as a militant leader, sought conflict and gloried in publicity and personal notoriety, his Irish-Catholic colleague on the Board of Regents displayed no need for that brand of self-indulgence. McEnerney was reserved, avoided public display, and guarded the privacy of his personal and intellectual life. From his behavior as a Regent it would seem that his sense of fulfillment came from skillful

114

participation in the management of the affairs of a large and growing institution, an institution with which his identity merged.

McEnerney's ability to identify himself so closely with the University of California, while Yorke could not, is explainable in part by their divergent temperaments, also by their very different backgrounds, which of course cannot be separated from the former. McEnerney was separated from Yorke in age only by a few months, being born in 1865. Unlike Yorke, though, he was American born and unlike most American Irish of the day, McEnerney's early years were spent in an agricultural rather than an urban-industrial environment. His youth was not associated with a Fulton Fish Market or a South of Market setting. In later life he could reminisce about his farm boy youth in Napa, California.[5]

When young Garret did come to the big city, he did not seek employment in the building trades or among the teamsters. Instead he looked to the advancement of his education. He came from a small farm, managed by a strong-willed mother, to the struggling young St. Mary's College which was still located in San Francisco. In 1881 St. Mary's conferred the Bachelor of Science degree upon him. His age, sixteen, plus the curriculum and instruction available during those early years, needless to say, were in great contrast to what later became the ingredients for a bachelor's degree. Considering the time and place, his educational attainments did introduce him to upward mobility.

McEnerney placed great value on higher education and spoke out strongly in its behalf prior to becoming a Regent. By 1895 he considered the era of the self-made man to be ending. Had successful men of the past had the benefits of advanced educations then their achievements would have been, he felt, even greater.[6] In his own case professional success, and all its economic, social, and cultural accompaniments, seemed linked more to the opportunities available in an expanding society, and the personal abilities of a very intelligent young man to continually develop his own talents in pace with, or a bit in advance of, such opportunities.

McEnerney's own study for the legal profession was not within the institutional structure of a law department. After his St. Mary's years, he returned to his home county and from age seventeen prepared for admission to the bar. On his twenty-first birthday, Wednesday, February 17, 1886, he stood in open court and was orally examined on his knowledge of the law before the local Superior Court Judge, the County Sheriff, and County Clerk.[7] That day there began a legal career destined to span fifty-six years of active practice which would bring a full and happy life, local prestige and international recognition. When that life ended a colleague could state that in his last twenty years of practice Garret McEnerney had been accorded a place of eminence given no other attorney of his generation.[8]

But for one basic difference, the same words could be said of Yorke in his calling. Yorke's place of eminence was accorded him primarily by a popular following. McEnerney had no mass following. His stature was recognized by judges, lawyers and men of larger affairs.

As a human being McEnerney possessed characteristics which would attract most people and in fact his death, even at advanced years, left a deep sense of loss among his associates. By unanimous consent he was a warmhearted gentleman in his personal and professional relationships, always courteous, gracious, and friendly. Snobbery and social barriers tended to amuse him, while sham and pretense repelled him. At the dinner table he was the happiest of conversationalists and to be seated next to him was automatically to be located next to the head of the table. His wit carried over to other sectors of his life. [9]

McEnerney's personal shyness or reserve was not the type arising from insufficient self-confidence. His interaction with his environment was quite satisfying to himself. He managed significant portions of that environment successfully and was well rewarded in return. He seems to have lived with all other portions in a well adjusted and comfortable manner. But unlike many of San Francisco's more flamboyant trial lawyers, McEnerney eschewed publicity. His satisfaction came from the substance of a transaction or interaction rather than from its appearance. "His offices, containing one of the finest private law libraries in existence, were characterized by monastic simplicity . . . ."[10] He disliked being interviewed, and on such rare occasions politely refused to discuss his role in major achievements. He wished instead to remain behind the scenes. [11]

His numerous and at times bountiful generosities to the University of California down through his forty-one years on the Board were secreted in anonymity. [12] His standard response to the never ending requests for expenditures not provided for in the annual University budget was personal contribution. Whether it was to satisfy the wishes of historian Herbert Bolton to acquire a Jesuit manuscript collection on sale in London, to enable a scholar to travel abroad for a foreign award, or to provide a gold watch for an old and loyal employee, McEnerney's response remained constant, "Please contribute for me any sum which is contributed by the other Regents and send me a memorandum of the amount."[13] Attached to his follow-up check would be a courteous gesture such as, "It gives me great pleasure to make the contribution."[14] On other occasions, he would assume the total expense. [15]

During the depression years for example, when attandance was low, he became a heavy purchaser of California-Stanford football tickets even though he was not noted as a devotee of sport. And in the end he bequeathed $400,000 to the Regents of the University of California for construction purposes or scholarships for women. In addition half the residue of his estate was to go to the University. [16] He singled out University President Robert G. Sproul and his boy, Bob, for personal benefactions which were appreciated by Sproul, not so much because of the generous amount, but rather as "final evidence of an invaluable friendship" which they symbolized. [17]

Blessed with a keen mind McEnerney seemed able to reason in an orderly, sound, and highly expeditious manner. He had an extraordinary memory which, when combined with the hours he reserved for protracted study and research throughout his legal career, resulted in the creation of a very proficient professional. [18] He recognized the need for specialization of functions, and appreciated developments in other fields. Unlike Yorke, he placed a high value on the professional advice available within the University for the resolution of psychological problems.[19]

McEnerney's first contact with Berkeley personnel dated back at least to 1898, three years prior to his appointment as Regent, when he represented a professor in the case of a contested will.[20] At that same time he served as the attorney for both the San Francisco and California Boards of Health. Through the years he represented a wide variety of clients in California, the East and some living abroad. McEnerney was well connected with Washington, D.C., lawyers from 1907, and was retained by parties to cases before the United States Supreme Court. He also served as a Special Master for the U. S. Supreme Court, and refereed a dispute between the Federal Government and the State of Oregon over ownership of Oregon lakes.[21]

Following the San Francisco earthquake and fire of 1906 he served on the Relief Corporation,[22] and has been credited with originating the idea whereby control of the recovery program was transferred from the hands of the Schmitz administration and placed instead with committees.[23] Following that disaster he promoted the passage of legislation, popularly known as the McEnerney Act, which permitted the owners of real property to restore their titles which had been lost through the destruction of public records. He also defended successfully the validity of that legislation before the courts.

On occasion San Francisco's Hibernia Savings and Loan Society added McEnerney to its own stable of Irish barristers to defend its institutional interests in the local courts.[24] His most important and enduring contact with San Francisco's Irish-Catholic subculture, however, was through his position as attorney for the Catholic Church. One elder statesman of that Church believes McEnerney never once recommended any course of action which later turned out to have been unwise. He advised his Archbishops on contracts and other legal matters through the years during which the Catholic Church of the San Francisco Archdiocese was being physically constructed.[25]

McEnerney's affiliations were quite orthodox through his life. He was an Irishman who had attained professional status. His political affiliation remained Democratic and his religion was Catholicism. As a thirty-eight year old widower of international legal repute he was joined in marriage, in 1903, by his Archbishop and appreciative client, Patrick Riordan, to Genevieve Green Hamilton.[26] Thirty-nine years later he was laid to rest by Riordan's successor, Archbishop John J. Mitty, who celebrated the solemn requiem for one of his Church's distinguished sons.[27] In attendance also were members of the Saint Mary's College Alumni Association who mourned the passing of a very illustrious graduate[28] who linked them to their historic academic origins. Between these dates, the Catholic University of American had conferred upon McEnerney an honorary doctorate.

His most noted single achievement was as an attorney in the service of Archbishop Riordan and the Catholic Church in California. This Church held a claim against the government of Mexico dating back to the time of Spanish and Mexican rule.[29] In 1875 an international claims commission had awarded the California bishops $904,000 which Mexico paid in gold by installments. This satisfied only part of the claim. After much lobbying by the Church with successive administrations, Secretary of State John Hay took action. He pressured Mexico to submit the case to the Permanent Court of Arbitration established by The Hague Convention of 1899. As the hearing date approached Archbishop Riordan grew apprehensive. The attorney who had piloted the Church's claim through all the political, as well as legal difficulties since 1853, was now eighty-three years old. As the case's living expert he was unable to attend the arbitration because of health. That his partner had been retained more for political reasons than for his skill before the courts, did not reassure Riordan.

Secretary of State Hay insisted that the Archbishop should engage additional counsel, and once the Archbishop concurred with that advice, Hay recommended John Bassett Moore, who then occupied the chair of international law and diplomacy at Columbia University. Riordan, however, resisted this attracted suggestion preferring instead an active lawyer who was at his best in oral arguments before a court. To the case he assigned Garret McEnerney and his decisiveness, in retrospect, was justified. The tribunal awarded the Catholic Church in California $1,420,000 in Mexican silver and $43,000 annually thereafter. Following the favorable decision a protracted disagreement over legal fees ensued, during which time Riordan remained unshaken in his gratitude to McEnerney for filling the breach at the eleventh hour when all might otherwise have been lost. Within the contractual agreement in force with his older attorneys, Riordan compensated McEnerney well for his presentation before the international tribunal, much to the displeasure and expense of the oldsters.

In future years McEnerney defended the Church against interloping claimants and received favorable press coverage for his brilliance and performance in open court.[30]

McEnerney-Yorke Relations

Father Yorke followed the career of the Church's attorney to the point of saving newspaper clippings concerning his accomplishments. As to the quality of their personal relationship during Yorke's years as a Regent, few landmarks are available. McEnerney was an individualist but functioned well within an institutional structure, so well that he manipulated the institution rather than simply performing in a predetermined role. Yorke on the other hand, as a militant leader, chafed under institutional restrictions. But like so many Irishmen in America he respected McEnerney's calling. He respected those who made the law, enforced it, and interpreted it. For Yorke's subculture, the quickest avenues along which advancement was possible for the talented were the Church, politics, and law. Yorke shared this pervasive view and while he credited manual labor as noble, he, nonetheless, knew that the Irish ditch digger did not care who dug tomorrow's ditch. The Irishman dreamed of his son occupying a place on the bench and Yorke appreciated their aspiration.[31]

To pin down Yorke's views on McEnerney's calling more specifically is difficult because of his fluctuating and occasionally wild personal statements. He denounced the Irish trial judges in the San Francisco graft prosecution as political glad-handers. Yet he admired Superior Court Judge James V. Coffee, and congratulated him on the twenty-fifth anniversary of his court appointment. Furthermore, Yorke approved of his active participation in Democratic politics while on the bench.[32] In all likelihood such participation was less important to Yorke than their respective orientations relative to local issues. Yorke was immersed in local politics himself. The norm drew the Irish barrister to politics rather than to corporate affairs or scholarship and contemplation. In this sense McEnerney's career pattern deviated from the standard Irish pattern. He cultivated no Irish societies, sought no local or state office. Also, he was not satisfied that legal decisions handed down by Judge Coffee, the jurist Yorke admired, were technically correct.[33]

Other individuals and concepts, serving as points of reference or orientation, indicate wide areas of disagreement between Yorke and McEnerney. In time McEnerney became a warm personal friend of Hiram Johnson, the graft prosecutor, Progressive California Governor, and United States Senator.[34] The two engaged in extended political correspondence through the 1930's and, in retrospect, McEnerney recommended that his friend stand on his lengthy record as a "liberal and a Progressive."[35] Yorke, it might be recalled, had opposed Johnson's brand of liberalism and Progressivism, and he abominated the graft prosecution. McEnerney shared the Progressive's notion of the urban political boss. He pictured such a being as immoral and devoid of all honor, as were the pretenders to respectability with whom they dealt -- politicians of the lower order.[36]

McEnerney also got on well with the younger Chester Rowell when he served as a Regent of the University of California.[37] Rowell was the Progressive leader considered by Yorke to have been a parasite on the body politic.

Of those who gather to memorialize Father Yorke each Palm Sunday, few know of Garret W. McEnerney. Those who do filter their knowledge of him through the Yorkean myth. To them McEnerney is but another self-designated high brow who had been reduced to humility by their champion of the common man. McEnerney and Yorke met each other directly over but one issue, American participation in World War I. The issue of the war and patriotism was causing internal and external problems for the University. For McEnerney and Yorke the question of America's response to the European conflict and their personal adjustment to the national effort was complicated by the fate of Ireland. Yorke was devoted to the cause of Irish independence and reasoned that England's preoccupation with Germany on the continent was Ireland's best chance to obtain its freedom. After the war's end, England would again have a free hand with which to deal with rebellious Ireland.

Yorke's war views were almost solely determined by his anti-British sentiments. During these years, for example, a strong letter of recommendation to Yorke from a friend included the fact that the Irishman being put forward as a new editor for Yorke's Leader was wanted by the British on the charge of High Treason. The charge grew out of his possession of homemade hand grenades, dynamite, rifles and automatic pistols while in Ireland.[38]

McEnerney's conscious decision was generally to avoid embroilment in issues over which a population divided. His advice for the University was to remain aloof in questions of a controversial nature even when fixed convictions were based on prejudice. He believed it would be better in the long run, and less perilous, to be concerned with doing useful work in noncontroversial areas. He felt only "rare occasions and unique combinations of circumstances may give rise to exceptions . . . ."[39] His general advice that the University let most fights pass by was used as a guide to his own personal behavior as well. His sense of restraint gave way in 1918, however. The patriotism of part of the University community was being questioned in the wake of the war effort and the concomitant suppression of intellectual deviation. Also, the Irish-Catholic population, which identified itself with Yorke's leadership, supported revolutionary activities in Ireland against England who was, at that time, America's partner in war against the Central Powers.[40]

McEnerney must have considered this combination of circumstances unique enough and the occasion a rare one, for on the evening of April 1, 1918, the tender of institutions stepped out of character and into the foreground of public conflict. On that evening he introduced T. P. O'Connor at a banquet held in his honor. O'Connor was a member of the British House of Commons. The main thrust of McEnerney's lengthy introduction argued that since the United States was then at war with Germany in the company of Great Britain, America's safety was the prime consideration. From this he concluded that any support given in America to any movement in Ireland, the object of which was to reduce Britain's ability to fight on the continent, was treasonable. As a corollary he reasoned that any attack in America on British attempts to maximize her fighting ability was also treasonable. Support of Irish-Americans for the Sinn Fein party in revolutionary Ireland amounted, in McEnerney's opinion, to "disaffection, disloyalty and treason." The reason he so concluded was because Sinn Fein sought British defeat at the hands of Germany while the United States fought for a British victory.[41]

Within the week delegates from sixty-four local Irish societies convened and soundly denounced the views presented by McEnerney. The acting chairman, Walter McGovern, recognized McEnerney as a prominent attorney but labeled him an expert out of his field. On the Irish question he was simply uninformed, and a possible reason for this could have been his failure to affiliate himself with any of the Irish societies. Beyond this, there was at least a hint of alienation which might now be called Uncle Tomism. McGovern felt that McEnerney's statement betrayed his lack of empathy for the "aspirations of the race he claims as his own."[42] He had become too assimilated. He had passed over.

McEnerney's torrid rejoinder flatly recommended that Irish aliens from twenty-one to thirty-one be drafted into military service and that others be deported. He questioned the loyalty of the United Irish Societies to America and recommended that they work for pacification of Ireland in order to free the English army of occupation for service against Germany. This was his test of their loyalty to America.[43]

Yorke's tolerance for rival points of view was admittedly low, and here, despite protestations to the contrary, he was unrestrained. As might be reasonably expected, he refused to recognize McEnerney as an authority on American patriotism and as an acceptable judge of Irish affairs.[44] From there he descended to personal invective, blended with anti-intellectualism. He appealed to the clear thinking of "the man in the street" to validate his point of view. And besides, the Irish societies had consulted legal opinion on the matter "every whit as capable as your learned self," Yorke asserted. Yorke's appeal was to his popular following and he rejected McEnerney's views, in part, by abusing him personally. Yorke's "Plain people" were the real ones and the "learned self" did not qualify for membership. McEnerney belonged instead with "the rich, the influential, the men of the class to which you have so laboriously attained," the class that gave only a "cheap sneer" to the cause of Irish freedom.[45] McEnerney may have been American born, to this Yorke would admit, but the body was only part of a human being, he maintained, and the lower part at that. Spiritually Mc Enerney was not an American at all, Yorke argued, since the nation was born of idealism and all his law books and ledgers were devoid of idealism. Sinn Feinners were the men of ideals and therefore true Americans supported them. Before retreating into the poetry of an executed Irish patriot, Yorke denounced McEnerney as the possessor of a "practical mind" concerned with the "star of success" alone.[46]

The heart of Yorke's reply was a syllogistic gyration in which he reformed the McEnerney statements into formal premises and conclusions. He then laboriously used what was then in fact his own formulation, to demonstrate that McEnerney was the actual traitor to America and not the Irish.

In what he dubbed McEnerney's "Theorem No. 3," Yorke stated as a major premise, "Anything that weakens the efficiency of the British forces in the war is treason to the United States." Yorke's minor was, "But the absence of conscription in Irelands [sic] weakens the efficiency of the British forces in the war." The logically required, if highly dubious, conclusion followed.

British conscription in Ireland received scarce support indeed. The most pro-British position was entertained by the old and withering Irish Nationalist party to which McEnerney's banquet guest belonged. Sinn Feinn violently opposed all Irish participation in the war. T. P. O'Connor's Nationalists opposed a British draft in Ireland but supported a vigorous campaign for voluntary participation by Irishmen in the English army. Even though he advocated a pro-British position with little support in Ireland, still he did not champion a draft. This enabled Yorke to push his syllogism even further. Since O'Connor opposed conscription in Ireland, he was therefore guilty of treason to the United States and it supposedly followed that "Mr. Garret McEnerney of San Francisco . . . backing up Mr. T. P. O'Connor . . . . therefore . . . is responsible for treason to the United States."[47]

In his conclusion Yorke abandoned the strained logic and again appealed to the masses. He wielded a body blow of questionable latitude, and placed the American flag and the honored dead with himself in juxtaposition to the learned self. "This very day," he declared,

I draped the American flag over the empty coffin of one of our lads whose bones repose on the field of honor "over there." These are the boys that in my ministry of over a generation . . . I begot unto Christ in Baptism, these are the boys I prepared for their First Communion and Confirmation, these are the boys whose sacred confidences I received . . . is there any man so heartless as to believe that my people or I would for a hundred Irelands or ten thousand Germanys do or say or even think anything that would harm a hair of their heads -- they who are bone of our bone and flesh of our flesh, our joy and our crown?[48]

Had Yorke restricted his assault on McEnerney to his own strained syllogisms, he would have displayed himself, in retrospect, as either a knave or a buffoon but for another important consideration. Yorke never felt any need to defent the University of California against any outside attack, indeed, he lead the first assault. Certainly loose charges of insufficient patriotism on the part of the University did not worry him as they did McEnerney. The Irish question complicated the adjustment or response of both Yorke and McEnerney to the war. Both were Irish, both fond of the fact but in different ways and to different degrees. Both had to deal with conflicting demands. What seemed best for America and best for Ireland at that time were not the same.

McEnerney, cognizant of the problem of the University, resolved the dilemma in his own mind by choosing what appeared to be one alternative. America's safety should be sought, and if this mitigated against Irish aspirations, this would be unfortunate but necessary. Realizing one cannot be on both sides of a divisive issue, he acted decisively and chose one side. Not being a man used to personal participation in the public arena of political controversy, he overreacted to the rejection of his point of view by the Irish-American subculture.

Peter Yorke on the other hand personally embodied the dilemma confronting his subculture. He could not turn his back on either Ireland or America. As most immigrants Yorke felt he had to be more loyal to the United States than the natives themselves. He had lived through difficult years when being a Catholic opened him to the charge of being anti-American. No Irishman wanted to repeat this experience, least of all Yorke.

He responded to the dilemma by trying to reconcile in his own mind two patterns of behavior which others viewed as incompatible. As Americans, for his subculture to support the national war effort was correct. Not only were they fighting for the United States, but he convinced himself, they fought for Ireland too. He preached this even though rebellion in Ireland kept some British troops from the front, resulting possibly in more empty coffins in St. Peter's parish. Yorke's inability to choose when choice seemed required forced him to accept this fiction -- the war was both for America and Ireland. If he needed any encouragement to accept such a fiction, President Woodrow Wilson provided it in his Fourteen Points -- self-determination for subject nations.

Once convinced himself, Yorke influenced his following in the belief that the lives of their sons lost in France were sacrificed that America remain safe and Ireland become free. Yorke shared this self-inflicted, beguiling delusion in order that he live in peace with himself, while behaving in the only manner possible given his basic assumptions. Not sharing these assumptions, McEnerney chose a different pattern of response, and judging from the starkness of his reaction to criticism, he lacked sufficient insight into the mind of the subculture to which he ostensibly belonged.

McEnerney's successful career in a field admired by the Irish had made him potentially influential over the Irish-Catholic mind. His lack of intimate contact with that mentality as it existed caused him to lose any influence he might have had. As a result he became alienated from the mass. And as so often was the case, Yorke fulfilled his accustomed function by administering the <u>coup</u> <u>de</u> <u>grâce</u>.

McEnerney's Response to Duty

Considering his treatment at the public forum, one can appreciate McEnerney's preference for the court room where the rules were clearly recognized, or for the tending of institutions in conference with a limited number of associates. McEnerney enjoyed being a Regent of the University of California and got on well with those interested in promoting its well-being. At the end of his third appointed term in 1936 President Robert G. Sproul actively lobbied for another sixteen year appointment.[49] A number of University supporters, which included seven Regents, petitioned the Governor in order that McEnerney be retained on the Board.[50] At his death six years later, one colleague regretted that "the meetings of the finance committee of the Board of Regents of the University of California seem strange assemblages without him."[51] President Sproul mourned the passing of one he considered as a wise and conscientious counselor, and "an understanding friend of faculty, students and administration." Sproul characterized him as a harmonizer of divergent opinion, "a unifying force in all University affairs."[52]

His entire approach to the University and its affairs, was characterized by basic assumptions which stand out in sharp relief to those of Yorke. McEnerney saw California as no threat to his values. Higher education was necessary for individuals to function best in the new century.[53] The University was well-suited to fulfill this need and, through his efforts, might do even better. If religion were a divisive subject, McEnerney was content to ignore it in the exercise of his functions as a Regent, and to let every man have his own private views as he certainly had his. When denominational advocates crossed the Berkeley campus and even participated in official functions, he neither encouraged nor discouraged them. He certainly did not view them as any serious threat to the Catholic Church or Catholic students.

In McEnerney's mind what went on at the University harmonized with his concept of the good society. Therefore the expansion and development of the institution in a careful and orderly manner was to the advantage of the state and its citizens. For a young boy or girl to attend the University was good, for more to attend was better. In this way McEnerney behaved like his fellow ethnics who controlled the hierarchy of the Catholic Church. He too was an organizer, expander, builder. Yorke deviated from the norm of Irish-Catholic leaders by not being an organization man. For that reason he was not advanced in the Catholic Church. McEnerney deviated by being detached from the working class character of Irish-Catholicism. For that reason he spoke infrequently to the subculture, and when he did he was stigmatized as an alien.

At the time of his first appointment as a Regent in 1901, the State of California was controlled by the northern section, most specifically by San Francisco. Then the University served as little more than a community institution. By the end of his Regency in 1942, the world had changed and so too had the political and demographic realities of his state. Through these years McEnerney had regularly opposed the elitist tendency of the Berkeley campus and those who held to it as their only love. He favored greater representation from the south on the Board of Regents.[54] He favored the development of the University of California at Los Angeles, and protected administrators on the southern campus. While seeking greater state support for the Los Angeles campus, he sternly resisted nonetheless the attempt of the state legislature to trade special appropriations for the ability to dictate on academic matters.[55] Arguments by Berkeleyites that teaching the same courses at the Los Angeles campus, while they were being taught at Berkeley, would erode the academic standard, had no effect on him.[56] His own enrapture with the Berkeley campus is demonstrated by the provisions of his will. Still if it were good for a San Francisco lad to attend Berkeley, the same desirable ends would be served by enabling more young persons throughout the state to have easier access to the same type of benefits -- locally.

Yorke's behavior regarding higher education generally and California in particular have already been examined. Periodically he advocated advanced education in his paper, but more often he discredited such institutions and their professors. He used the learned scholar as a convenient symbol with which to manipulate the emotions of his working class following. Such a symbol attracted and repelled simultaneously. For Yorke to disparage McEnerney as a learned self was no more difficult than to wrap the advocacy of Gaelic study in the aura of President Wheeler's scholarship or reader O' Hegarty's University of California methodology. Totally missing from the records of Regent Yorke's relationship with the University of California is any hint that he felt it would be good for the children of his subculture to attend this institution.

In glaring contrast, when one opens the first foler of the McEnerney manuscripts contained within the archives of the University of California, one immediately finds that the recently approved Regent began what was to become an enduring personal policy of urging the admission if individual students. His interests ranged over the field of under-graduate scholarships to medical internships. These were personal letters between Regent McEnerney and the various administrators which endured through the years.[57] In contrast to Yorke, McEnerney's behavior indicated he placed high value on a California degree and was anxious that young people avail themselves of the educational opportunities. Obviously he did not feel that knowing a Regent barred one from seeking admission or even financial assistance through him. Those requests which filtered through his hands were either personally supported or simply passed on as received. All his efforts were not successful. Never did he treat these requests as high priority matters, and never did he react strongly to the outcomes. He simply supported the legitimate applications of prospective students with varying degrees of personal enthusiasm, and then allowed the administration to react as it saw fit. Being a highly perceptive individual, McEnerney could hardly have considered his influence unimportant.

McEnerney was not above prompting faculty selection also, at least during the beginning of his Regency.[58] In that day the University had not yet passed the lift-off point of academic renown and the new, young Regent apparently felt free to make such a suggestion. In future years he never behaved so boldly in this area. When he later concerned himself with faculty personnel matters his efforts were in behalf of faculty welfare, retention, and safeguards against arbitrary treatment at administrative hands.[59]

On the questions of faculty pensions he was liberal, but only to the point of what he considered needed safeguards to the integrity of the institution. President Wheeler was very anxious at one time to bring the University's retirement program into line with the pension directives of the Carnegie Foundation in order to protect himself from personnel raids by Eastern schools which already enjoyed Carnegie support.[60] McEnerney objected to the degree of influence exercised by the Foundation over institutions of higher learning which accepted its pension grants and displayed no desire that the same should happen to California.[61] Beyond this McEnerney wished that the age of retirement should be more at the discretion of the University rather than the individual professor.[62] Within these limits he advanced the well-being of faculty members.

Regent Yorke's attitude toward the Carnegie retirement funds provoked his public scorn since Catholic institutions and their professors were not included within the provisions as determined by the Foundation.[63] His fumings were public, however, and as a Regent he never concerned himself with the matter as it related to the University, in spite of the fact that Carnegie money was also available to the Lick Observatory, suppossedly his major area of concern as a member of the Lick committee. Wheeler simply bypassed Yorke, following the truism that sleepy dogs not be kicked, especially ones whose temperaments were uneven. Wheeler manipulated the circumstances so as to obtain access to Carnegie moneys for the University in such a way that Regent McEnerney would favor. This meant negotiating with the foundation director and with McEnerney. Peter Yorke was not a factor to be considered in the resolution of the problem. His withdrawal from the problem was one way he avoided the inevitable dilemma of redefining the constituency he served as a Regent.

Consistent with his basic assumption that higher education was desirable and Berkeley was no threat, McEnerney generally favored expansion of the University at the same time that he encouraged upgrading the quality of the education being offered. As the years passed and the basic undergraduate sector of the University matured, he favored greater efforts in areas of professional education and the auxiliary services which surround well-ordered adult institutions. He favored the establishment of the student hospital and improved medical education.[64] The limitations he placed on such expansions were conditioned by his expectations of what the taxpayers of the state might be willing to support. Even here though his inclination was towards expansion. He operated on the assumption that as long as no outrageous expenditures were made and University funds were well-managed, then the state would support ordered growth and development. This assumption was correct.

McEnerney identified himself so closely with the University that when commenting on what the institution should do to advance or protect itself, he would lapse into the first person plural. For McEnerney it was a question of what "we" should do for "our" protection and advancement.[65] Unlike Yorke, he did not envision the University as a separate, alien entity in relation to himself. How then could he fear or distrust it?

Committee work consumed much of the time McEnerney devoted to University affairs. Through his lengthy Regency he did serve on less exciting committees. Such was the exception though. From the start of his official relationship with the University he was uniquely situated so as to be of distinct advantage to the institution. As a Regent he sat on the endowment committee, while at the same time served as executor and attorney of record for large estates, portions of which were bequeathed to the University of California.[66] Occasionally McEnerney voted against the distribution of committee assignments, and even against the very existence of committees to which he was subsequently appointed.[67] Still, he always served. His colleagues periodically chose him for membership on the Committee on Committees. At the end of his career he served on the Finance Committee, and the Jurisprudence Committee which he chaired, in addition to being Chairman of the Board of the Regents of the University of California. In the interim the University acquired the Bancroft Library while he served on the Library and Museum Committee.[68] He was personally generous towards the Lick Observatory and its personnel in his affluent years after he had served on that committee.[69]

The early records of meetings held by the Regents of the University of California are characterized by brevity and formality. Through the forty-one years McEnerney served on the Board the minute books progressed from stylish but difficult to read script, to typed summaries, and ending with verbatum transcripts. In the last stage a "hard" data researcher would be able to plot how discussion leaned toward McEnerney's end of the table. In the qualitative sense he dominated too. He could rephrase seemingly conflicting proposals to mutual satisfaction.[70] Only on the rarest of occasions before 1912, however, did the arid records include sufficient information to determine where a divisive issue existed, what were the sides, and who advocated what.

McEnerney's attendance clearly illustrates his serious interest in the University. Again in contrast to his colleague, he attended meetings regularly while carrying on a career every bit as full as Father Yorke's. Also, unlike Yorke, he kept the Board and the President regularly informed of his whereabouts. He was willing to arrange his private business so as to accommodate the demands of the University,[71] and when a court appearance or Eastern clients required his presence, the apologetic note explaining his forthcoming absence found its way to Berkeley.[72] During his absence, correspondence from the University was promptly attended to by his law office staff. For Garret McEnerney, missing a University of California Regents' meeting required an explanation. This practiced behavior sprang from more than merely good manners. During his absence colleagues would defer important University discussions awaiting his return.[73] At the meetings his motions referred matters back to committee, entrusted them to the attorney of the Regents with power to act, or referred them to the President to be resolved at his discretion.[74] As a perceptive and attentive Regent he could anticipate what action would then be taken or not taken.

Moments of temporary crisis or indecision reached out for McEnerney's guidance. As early as 1904, President Wheeler asked, as a personal favor to himself, that McEnerney be present when a Regents' committee met with members of the medical faculty. The topic of discussion was a University hospital. Sides were drawn and Wheeler believed the matter represented "so important a crisis in the affairs of our Medical Department that I should be personally very much indebted to you if you could come."[75] In matters of confidence and personnel concerning the Regents themselves, Presidents were opened to McEnerney and sought his advice while they kept others in the dark.[76]

Fellow Regents sought McEnerney's advice when they approached important undertakings, as when the Finance Committee considered the purchase of the Bancroft Library in 1905. That committee was ably chaired by veteran Regent Arthur Foster. Though McEnerney was not a member, the committee requested that he join them in Foster's San Francisco office to consider such an important matter.[77] McEnerney advised from behind the scenes on other crucial matters, such as the tenure of Presidents and their relationship to the Regents, faculty, and other administrative officers. He was precise, forceful, and reasonable.[78]

By virtue of his stature within the legal profession and his willingness always to be of service to the University, McEnerney found himself being drafted as somewhat of a super lawyer for California. The Regents of the University of California retained their own attorney who tended the legal affairs of the institution. On important or delicate matters McEnerney would serve with a committee of lawyers from the Board, or more often as an individual would instruct the University's attorney on how he should proceed.[79] He never took the initiative in such situations, but always served eagerly once called, as in the case of the Kearney will. Theodore Kearney had bequeathed to the University extensive landholdings and an agricultural syndicate in the Central Valley. At the time McEnerney was occupied in court himself every day amid rival claims to another large estate, but he still responded to Wheeler's fears for the University in his typical manner. Reassuring the President he wrote:

> I am prepared . . . (without charge, of course), to contribute any service I may be able to render, and perform any labor which may be assigned to me by you, by Mr. Snook [attorney for the Regents] or by the committee of lawyers of the Board, in defense of Mr. Kearney's will.[80]

As a Regent of the University of California, Garret McEnerney seems ideal from the institutional vantage point. He was very intelligent, talented, well-respected, balanced, and deliberative in outlook and behavior. He had no strong fixations and functioned effectively atop a sea of personal good will.

[1] James P. Gaffey, The Life of Patrick William Riordan: Second Archbishop of San Francisco, 1841-1914 (Ph.D. dissertation, Catholic University of America, 1965), p. 328.

[2] The Monitor, (San Francisco), Dec. 28, 1951.

[3] Garret W. McEnerney to E. D. Coblents, San Francisco, Mar. 6, 1937, Hiram Johnaon MSS, Bancroft Library, Berkeley; John F. Neylan to McEnerney, San Francisco, Jan. 3, 1941, Neylan MSS, Bancroft Library; McEnerney to Luther A. Nichols, San Francisco, Sept. 18, 1936, McEnerney MSS AUC; McEnerney to A. Dana Hodgdon, San Francisco, Mar. 24, 1931, Willard H. Durham MSS, Bancroft Library, Berkeley.

[4] Peter C. Yorke, America and Ireland: An Open Letter to Mr. Garret W. McEnerney (San Francisco: Text Book Publishing, 1918), appendix.

[5] John F. Neylan, a biographical sketch of Garret W. McEnerney in Neylan, MSS, Bancroft Library, Berkeley.

[6] Oscar T. Shuck, ed., History of the Bench and Bar of California (Los Angeles: Commercial Printing House, 1901), pp. 638, 641.

[7] "Admission of Garrett [sic] W. McEnerney to the practice of law, California Superior Court, Napa Co.," certified copy, C-Y 18, Bancroft Library, Berkeley.

[8] Neylan biographical sketch of McEnerney in Neylan MSS, Bancroft Library, Berkeley.

[9] William G. Bradley to John F. Neylan, New York, Aug. 5, 1942; John P. Coghlan to Neylan, San Francisco, Jan. 12, 1943; W. L. McGinness, Jr. to Neylan, Tegucigalpa, Honduras, Jan. 15, 1943; Neylan to R. M. Tobin, San Francisco, Jan. 15, 1943, Neylan MSS, Bancroft Library, Berkeley; Regent's minutes, Aug. 8, 1933, in Charles A. Ramm, MSS CU-5 Box 319, AUC.

[10] Neylan biographical sketch of McEnerney in Neylan MSS, Bancroft Library, Berkeley.

[11] Bob Henderson, "Oldest Regent Has Watched College Grow," Daily Californian, Mar. 26, 1942; Shuck, op.cit., p. 638.

[12] McEnerney to Robert G. Sproul, San Francisco, Dec. 31, 1935, McEnerney MSS AUC.

[13] McEnerney to Wheeler, San Francisco, April 17, 1905, McEnerney MSS AUC.

[14]McEnerney to Wheeler, San Francisco, April 27, 1905, McEnerney MSS AUC.

[15]Neylan biographical sketch of Garrett W. McEnerney in Neylan MSS, Bancroft Library, Berkeley.

[16]Undated memorandum CU-5, Box 592, McEnerney MSS AUC.

[17]Robert G. Sproul to Garret McEnerney II, Berkeley, April 24, 1943, McEnerney MSS AUC.

[18]Neylan biographical sketch of McEnerney in Neylan MSS, Bancroft Library, Berkeley.

[19]Walter Morris Hart to McEnerney, Sept. 18, 1925, McEnerney MSS AUC.

[20]McEnerney to George Davidson, San Francisco, Sept. 13, 1898; Jan. 19, 1901, Davidson MSS, Bancroft Library, Berkeley.

[21]McEnerney to Wheeler, San Francisco, May 4, 1908; Sept. 9, 1906, McEnerney MSS AUC; McEnerney to Hiram Johnaon, San Francisco, June 6, 1937, McEnerney to Johnson, San Francisco, Dec. 1, 1932; May 25, 1931; Oct. 30, 1931, Hiram Johnson MSS, Bancroft Library, Berkeley.

[22]McEnerney to Wheeler, San Francisco, Aug. 18, 1906, McEnerney MSS AUC.

[23]Peter C. Yorke, America and Ireland . . . , p. 22; Walton Bean, Boss Ruef's San Francisco: The Story of the Union Labor Party, Big Business, and the Graft Prosecution (Berkeley: University of California, 1952), p. 121.

[24]"Notice to Produce," Superior Court of California (SF), No. 255003, Neylan MSS, Bancroft Library, Berkeley.

[25]Statement made by Monsignor Harold Collins in an interview, San Francisco, June 4, 1969.

[26]Wedding Certificate, Garret W. McEnerney and Genevieve Green Hamilton, C-H 67, Bancroft Library, Berkeley.

[27]Berkeley Daily Gazette, Aug. 5, 1942.

[28]Examiner (San Francisco), Aug. 5, 1942.

[29]For the history of the case see Garret W. McEnerney, "Pious Fund of the Californias," The Catholic Encyclopedia, XII (1912), pp. 106-7; William E. McDonald, "The Pious Fund of the Californias," The Catholic Historical Review, XIX (Jan., 1934), pp. 427-36; Gaffey, op.cit., pp. 265-355.

[30]"Paten Book" containing clippings from the Los Angeles Examiner, Yorke Collection, AUSF.

[31]The Leader, Jan. 4, 1908.

[32]Ibid., Feb. 1, 1908.

[33]McEnerney to Wheeler, San Francisco, Mar. 27, 1905, McEnerney MSS AUC.

[34]McEnerney to Hiram Johnson, San Francisco, Sept. 1, 1930, Johnson MSS, Bancroft Library, Berkeley.

[35]McEnerney to Johnson, San Francisco, telegram, Aug. 3, 1940, Johnson MSS, Bancroft Library, Berkeley.

[36]McEnerney to Johnson, San Francisco, Mar. 26, 1937, Neylan MSS, Bancroft Library, Berkeley.

[37]McEnerney to Chester Rowell, San Francisco, Sept. 2, 1928, Rowell MSS, Bancroft Library, Berkeley.

[38]John Devoy to Yorke, New York, Oct. 6, 1915, Yorke Collection, AUSF.

[39]McEnerney to Wheeler, San Francisco, July 3, 1914, McEnerney MSS AUC.

[40]For a detailed analysis of American Catholicism related to the European war prior to the United States entry see Edward Cuddy, "Pro-Germanism and American Catholicism, 1914-1917," The Catholic Historical Review, LIV (Oct., 1968), pp. 427-454. It should be noted that the Catholic press here sampled did not include Yorke's Leader which was rabidly pro-Irish in relation to the official Archdiocesan Monitor which was classified on the issue of war as "Neutral but with muted sympathy for Germany," A reason why it could be so classified could be that the less moderate Irish-Catholics of San Francisco were drawn off in support of Yorke's unofficial weekley.

[41]Peter C. Yorke, America and Ireland . . . , appendix.

[42]Loc. cit.

[43]Loc. cit.

[44]Ibid., pp. 48-50.

[45]Ibid., p. 8.

[46]Ibid., p. 33.

[47] Ibid., p. 40.

[48] Ibid., pp. 48-50.

[49] J. P. Chandler to Robert G. Sproul, Los Angeles, April 8, 1936; Byron Hanna to Sproul, Los Angeles, April 10, 1936, McEnerney MSS AUC.

[50] Daily Californian, Mar. 19, 1936.

[51] John F. Neylan to William Gage Bradley, San Francisco, Aug. 11, 1942, Neylan MSS, Bancroft Library, Berkeley.

[52] Daily Californian, Aug. 4, 1942.

[53] Oscar T. Shuck, op.cit., p. 638.

[54] Regents of the University of California to Governor Frank F. Merriam, Berkeley, April 17, 1936, photostat, McEnerney MSS AUC.

[55] McEnerney to William W. Campbell, San Francisco, May 8, 1927, McEnerney MSS AUC; Regents' minutes, Aug. 8, 1933, in Charles A. Ramm MSS CU-5 Box 319 AUC.

[56] David P. Barrows to McEnerney, Berkeley, April 12, 1923, McEnerney, MSS AUC.

[57] For a sample see Secretary to the President to McEnerney, Berkeley, May 9, 1903; McEnerney to Wheeler, San Francisco, Aug. 1, 1904; Aug. 9, 1905; Aug. 3, 1907; R. M. Underhill to McEnerney, Berkeley, Jan. 13, 1933; Robert G. Sproul to McEnerney, Berkeley, Feb. 13, 1937, McEnerney MSS AUC.

[58] Wheeler to McEnerney, Berkeley, Aug. 9, 1902, McEnerney MSS AUC.

[59] William W. Campbell to McEnerney, Berkeley, April 7, 1928, McEnerney MSS AUC.

[60] Wheeler to McEnerney, Berkeley, Jan. 31, 1907, McEnerney MSS AUC.

[61] McEnerney to Wheeler, San Francisco, July 1, 1909, McEnerney MSS AUC.

[62] Wheeler to McEnerney, Berkeley, Feb. 25, 1905, McEnerney MSS AUC.

[63] The Leader, July 15, 1911.

[64] McEnerney to Wheeler, San Francisco, July 27, 1906; Aug. 25, 1910, McEnerney MSS AUC.

[65]McEnerney to Wheeler, San Francisco, Sept. 9, 1906; McEnerney to R. M. Underhill, San Francisco, Sept. 30, 1939, McEnerney MSS AUC.

[66]UC Regent's Minute Book, XIV, 50, 55-56, 213; V. Henderson to McEnerney, Berkeley, Feb. 13, 1904; Wheeler to McEnerney, Berkeley, May 13, 1903, McEnerney MSS AUC; Chronicle, Aug. 4, 1942.

[67]UC Regent's Minute Book, XIV, 253; XVI, 325.

[68]Ibid., XIV, 358; V. Henderson to Garret McEnerney, Berkeley, Nov. 15, 1905, McEnerney MSS AUC.

[69]UC Regent's Minute Book, XVI, 93, 194; XVII, 119.

[70]Ibid., XIV, 136; XVI, 219; XV, 123.

[71]McEnerney to Wheeler, San Francisco, Jan. 21, 1908, McEnerney MSS AUC.

[72]McEnerney to Wheeler, San Francisco, Sept. 9, 1906, May 4, 1908; McEnerney to Victor H. Henderson, San Francisco, Mar. 20, 1911, McEnerney MSS AUC.

[73]UC Regent's Minute Book, XVI, 56.

[74]Ibid., XVI, 287, 326; McEnerney to Charles W. Slack, San Francisco, Jan. 11, 1924, McEnerney MSS AUC.

[75]Wheeler to McEnerney, Berkeley, Oct. 28, 1904; Dec. 21, 1904, McEnerney MSS AUC.

[76]Russ Avery to Robert G. Sproul, Los Angeles, Aug. 14, 1936; Sproul to Avery, Berkeley, Aug. 21, 1936; President's Secretary to McEnerney, Berkeley, Nov. 18, 1924, McEnerney MSS AUC.

[77]Victor Henderson to McEnerney, Berkeley, Nov. 6, 1905, McEnerney MSS AUC.

[78]McEnerney to James K. Moffitt, San Francisco, Jan. 3, 1923, Rowell MSS, Bancroft Library, Berkeley.

[79]Henderson to McEnerney, Berkeley, Jan. 15, 1904; Wheeler to McEnerney, Mar. 5, 1905; Wheeler to McEnerney, Sept. 4, 1906; William W. Campbell to McEnerney Feb. 20, 1924; May 19, 1928, McEnerney MSS AUC.

[80]McEnerney to Wheeler, San Francisco, Sept. 9, 1906, McEnerney MSS AUC.

CHAPTER IX

EPILOGUE

The most noted authority on the history of American Catholicism, John Tracy Ellis, frequently cites in his public lectures and published works the judgement of a Cambridge professor regarding the lack of intellectual prestige among American Catholics. In no other Western nation are Catholics held to be so powerful in terms of wealth, numbers, and superlative organization. But likewise, in no other Western nation is their intellectual prestige so low.[1] Ellis attributes this fact, in large part, to the Church's immigrant past. The avalanche of Catholic immigrants which descended upon the American Church in the nineteenth and early twentieth centuries preoccupied the Church hierarchy for generations. This situation, combined with the more pervasive nonintellectualism and at times anti-intellectualism found in America at large, mitigated against the formation of a strong intellectual environment within which Catholics might live. In addition, Catholics have been inhibited in their professional aspirations by blatant and the more subtle forms of religious discrimination.[2]

In commenting upon this interpretation Henry F. May, whose field is American intellectual history with specialization in American Protestantism, has cited other Catholic authors to the effect that their Church suffered from "formalism" and "Authoritarianism," terms which are defined as inhibitors of intellectual curiosity, as the tendency to see the world as complete or "finished." Accordingly it would seem that knowledge is rather fixed and final, rather than tentative, expanding, and elusive. May advanced the additional suggestion that American Catholics have found it difficult to carry on "a searching dialogue with non-Catholic American culture."[3] He did not speculate, however, on the relationship of his final suggestion, this lack of dialogue, to the immigrant background which Ellis held to be the vital consideration and May downgraded.

If in fact a difference in interpretation actually does exist between these two historians as to why Catholics have not shared in American intellectual life to the degree of the dominant culture, it may be conditioned by the scope of their respective areas of specialization. Unlike those by May, the early monographs of Ellis dealt with the Church in a foreign and in an international setting.[4] In any generalization he wishes to posit concerning American Catholicism, Ellis is confronted with the basic decision of whether such a generalization rests on what is unique to the Church in America or on what may be universal Catholic phenomena. If May's suggestions concerning "formalism" and "Authoritarianism" are not unique to American Catholicism but are equally valid when applied to the universal Church, then why has Catholic intellectual life in America been less vigorous than in other Western countries?

No resolution of this problem is actually promoted by an analysis of Yorke and the intellectual life. Rather than providing insights leading toward a solution, the Yorke case splendidly exemplifies the difficulties inherent in the problem. Peter C. Yorke embodied each and every one of the concepts which both Ellis and May have used in rival explanations of the relative lack of Catholic participation in American intellectual life. Yorke was every bit a child of the immigrant milieu. Circumstances drove him from Ireland. The immigrants' demand for priests secured him a berth in San Francisco where, for the remainder of his life, he looked back longingly to Ireland as one in forced exile. Yorke had disliked graduate studies, and later muckraked universities and their professors. If he did not suffer from religious discrimination personally, he was well aware of its existence through American history. His sensitivities to the problem, both real and exaggerated, were what brought him to initial public notice. Militancy, plus political connections, gave him his entrée to the Board of Regents of the University of California.

Additionally, Yorke did tend to see the world as complete and all things in it as obvious. If anyone else could not fathom its meaning and essence, Yorke, with supreme self-confidence, could always set such hesitant types straight -- even when they did not solicit such direction. Yorke operated on the assumption that Catholic doctrine, as he understood it, contained within its principles the solutions to all problems. Rather than attempting to resolve problems through the discovery of new knowledge, solutions resulted from the application of doctrine merely to novel situations.

Yorke was perpetually troubled by the relationship of religion to education, especially as it related to public education. He opposed the sectarianism of his day as a violation of the rights of Catholic parents and children under the Constitution. He opposed nonsectarianism on the same grounds when he considered it as simply a new sect, or else as a colossal fraud on religion in general. His intellectual response was aggravated by his firm conviction that religion was a basic element of all education for all people. Still he never could come to the point of maintaining that his own religion should be the one with which all children should be educated. The result was that out of a major concern of his life, he brought forth no satisfactory solution, nor did he even identify one.

Yorke's primary objection to the University of California, voiced in 1900, was that there was not a proportionate number of Catholics on the faculty and the Board of Regents. He viewed the institution not as a place where children of his subculture could obtain a first class education under state auspices, but rather as a place to acquire a government job. As the first ethnic militant to attack the University of California, and the only one to have been subsequently appointed to its governing body, posterity might be expected to look to him for some guidance on how such a dominant institution might be harmonized with a sector of the state's populace which was, in effect, beyond the University's consensus. Here again posterity looks in vain. He was unconcerned with bringing Catholic students to Berkeley. He was unconcerned with making Berkeley acceptable to Catholic students. In fact, he would prefer such students to remain away. He did nothing to reduce the sense of alienation within the Irish-Catholic-labor subculture. He had attacked the University Regents and administration for alleged discrimination, but once a Regent himself, he took no significant action in this regard, nor did he ever retract his charges.

From his behavior as a Regent it seems warranted to conclude that were it not for his sectarian/nonsectarian dilemma, he would have approved of the way the University functioned under Board direction. His own inability to enter into "a searching dialogue with non-Catholic American culture," as symbolized by the University of California, was provoked more by alienation from the club-church-reform mind which dominated Berkeley on the eve of Progressivism. After publicly denouncing the President as a "dangerous" man politically, he still stood and was counted among those who approved of Wheeler's transformation of Berkeley into a University in fact. What Yorke objected to was not how the institution was being managed, but rather who was doing the managing. From the vantage point of Berkeley the Regents and administrators may have been the "best people." From Yorke's perspective they were hardly "the real people."

Cultural considerations were more important than educational considerations for Yorke. Once on the inside, Yorke found that these subcultural predispositions were not unique guides for action. The other Regents, plus the administrators, were honest, sincere, and hard working human beings. No conspiracy existed to exclude Catholics. He discovered shortly enough that he himself lacked the basic skills required of a man to function well as a Regent. In his particular case he also lacked the appropriate psychological prerequisites to function at all in a secondary capacity while learning and developing such expertise. Given his own psychological make-up and the total situation in which he found himself, his response is understandable.

Peter C. Yorke as a Regent of the University is, nonetheless, the story of an opportunity lost. Obviously enough, Yorke did not work hard at solving educational problems for the University of California. Contrary to what has been claimed[5] Yorke did not serve any general interest regardless of race or creed. Just as the Berkeley reformers did, Yorke too served a special interest. His was Irish-Catholic-labor. Berkeley's was Angl-Protestant, white-collar. In retrospect his appointment as a Regent appears unfortunate. He did not advance the interests of the University. He did not accelerate or improve the institution's advance toward what it was already becoming, nor did he even attempt to redirect or reform it so as to serve the subculture with which he so closely identified.

No one profited by Yorke's tenure as a Regent, neither the University of California, his subculture, nor himself. His historical image is not enhanced by a vigorous analysis of his Regency. From start to finish the episode was one characterized by political gamesmanship and personal indulgence. His appointment was at the hands of a personal friend who had been denied the renomination of his political party. As a lame duck Governor, Henry Gage rewarded Yorke for past political service at the expense of education in California. Yorke's tenure did not graft Irish-Catholic-labor to the University as a new supporting constituency nor did it convert Yorke. Stanford University and the Catholic University of America survived Yorke's shafts and at much less cost than that paid by the University of California. California absorbed a critic who, once he became a member of the inner circle, once he had access to supposed institutional power, then did not know how to behave in order to effect his goals.

Yorke had been alienated from the hierarchy of his own institution, the Catholic Church. In 1900 he spoke as if official position on the Board of Regents was sufficient to direct or control University affairs and policies. He did not envision administration as an arena in which combat took place. He did not envision a Regent's commission as analogous to a hunting license which authorized its bearer to enter the game and try his luck. Once issued a license, Yorke declined to participate in the hunt.

He did not devote his Regency to the resolution of the problems inherent in the sense of alienation felt by a predominantly working class ethnic minority towards the leading institution of higher education in their locale. Such is quite understandable in that he felt their alienation was appropriate. Neither did he modify the institution to make it more open and acceptable to them. His behavior as a Regent likewise provided knowledgeable University personnel with no new insights which would more favorably dispose them toward Irish-Catholic-labor. From Yorke's first attack on the University through the period of his Regency ending in 1912, the percentage of degrees the University awarded to candidates which can be identified as Irish clearly declined. In 1900 the University conferred degrees on sixty-two young scholars having Irish family names. In 1912 the number increased to only seventy while the total number of degrees conferred increased from 328 to 543. During these years, a period of unprecedented university growth, the children of his subculture lost ground in relation to the total student population at Berkeley.[6]

Yorke was not, however, the only Irish-Catholic on the Board through this period. Garret McEnerney's obvious success as an attorney, a field much admired by the Irish, plus his official connection with the Catholic Archdiocese, placed him in a position of potential influence over subcultural thinking. He respected the value of higher education, saw California as a means by which young people could obtain such an education, and he worked to improve and expand such opportunities. To him the University was no threat to the Catholic Church or to Catholic children, so he assisted students to avail themselves of what the University offered.

One of the basic differences between Yorke and McEnerney was that the former gloried in publicity and conflict, while the latter preferred anonymity and harmony. Yorke courted the crowd while McEnerney enjoyed the solitude of his library and the company of close associates and friends. McEnerney was a man of large affairs conducted without pretense, and preferably away from public gaze. His effort at directing students to the University was of a typically private and personal nature, and therefore, very limited in scope and rather selective in terms of the socio-economic scale. McEnerney had no political ambitions and was not a habitué of Irish society socials. He cultivated no mass following and had none. His potential influence over the local Irish-Catholic mind was never actualized for the subculture's educational benefit. From his Regency the University accrued massive benefits, but his lack of popular influence over the subcultural mind prevented him from altering Irish-Catholicism's view of Berkeley.

Yorke could have served as a bridge to new intellectual vistas over which might have traveled the sons of union laborers. He had the popular influence within the sub-culture to do it. McEnerney's position was simply the reverse. The chasm between himself and the predominantly working class Irish enabled Yorke to totally discredit him in the popular mind. From then on, any advocacy by him of a California education would be additionally suspect because he was the one suggesting it. After his loyalty encounter with Yorke, he was unable to direct the flow of students out of San Francisco's Irish neighborhoods and into Berkeley even if he had been so inclined. He excelled as Regent, but did not effect the quality of Irish-Catholic-labor's intellectual aspirations. His influence on education was limited by the extermities of the very large institution he served so well.

Although Yorke was a failure as a Regent, the University of California was both sufficiently secure and mature to survive his Regency and, in fact, to continue advancing without him. A chronic absentee had no effect on policy. The tragedy of Yorke's appointment was not its effect on the University but rather its noneffect on his subculture. Rather than taking bright young lads from his parish school's science class on outings to the Lick Observatory and encouraging them in a field of Catholic neglect, he joined contemporary denunciation of "flunkey Catholics"[7] who sent their children on to universities of prestige.

As late as 1967 sufficient evidence existed to support the generalization that Catholic college students, when compared with non-Catholic college students, still were relatively uncommitted intellectually and close-minded.[8] These findings are highly consistent with the intellectual history of American Catholicism. Peter C. Yorke as a Regent of the University of California is very much a part of that history. As a well-placed ethnic leader, he allowed to pass a unique opportunity for fostering a commitment to scholarship. He rejected a unique chance to engage in a searching dialogue between Irish-Catholic-labor and the reform-minding non-Catholic culture which dominated Berkeley and the University of California. Instead he debased even further the quality of intellectual life within his own working class subculture.

NOTES CHAPTER IX

[1] D. W. Brogan, U.S.A.: An Outline of the Country, Its People and Institutions (London, 1941), p. 65, as cited in John Tracy Ellis, American Catholicism (Chicago: University of Chicago, 1956), p. 117.

[2] Ellis, American Catholicism, pp. 147-9.

[3] Henry F. May, "The Recovery of American Religious History," The American Historical Review, LXX (Oct. 1964), 91.

[4] Francis J. Weber, "John Tracy Ellis, Historian of American Catholicism," The American Benedictine Review, XVII (Winter, 1966), 467; John Tracy Ellis, Cardinal Consalvi and Anglo-Papal Relations, 1814-1824 (Washington, D.C.: Catholic University of America, 1942).

[5] Sister Mary C. Fitzmaurice, B.V.M., Historical Development of the Educational Thought of Reverend Peter C. Yorke, 1893-1925 (M.A. thesis, University of San Francisco, 1963), p. 10.

[6] An examination of the lists of those who were awarded degrees in 1900 and 1911-12 indicated the following ethnic information. Those with clearly identifiable Irish names amounted to 7% (1900) and 4.78% (1911-12). Those whose names were possibly Irish, 11.8% (1900) and 8.1% (1911-12). The lengthy checking of the ethnic derivation of these names was accomplished by Michael K. Tamoney, Assistant Court Commissioner, California Superior Court, City Hall, San Francisco.

[7] The Leader, Aug. 12, 1911, an editorial reprint from the Chicago New World.

[8] James W. Trent, Catholics in College -- Religious Commitment and the Intellectual Life (Chicago: University of Chicago, 1967), pp. 90-3, 207-9. See also Julian Foster, "Some Effects of Jesuit Education: A Case Study," in Robert Hassenger, ed., The Shape of Catholic Higher Education (Chicago: University of Chicago, 1967), pp. 163-90.

BIBLIOGRAPHY

MANUSCRIPTS

George Davidson Manuscripts, Bancroft Library, University of California, Berkeley, California.

William R. Davis Manuscripts, Bancroft Library, University of California, Berkeley, California.

William Denman Manuscripts, Bancroft Library, University of California, Berkeley, California.

Williard H. Durham Manuscripts, Bancroft Library, University of California, Berkeley, California.

Guy C. Earl Manuscripts, Bancroft Library, University of California, Berkeley, California.

Hiram Johnson Manuscripts, Bancroft Library, University of California, Berkeley, California.

William Carey Jones Manuscripts, Bancroft Library, University of California, Berkeley, California.

Garret W. McEnerney Manuscripts, Archives of the University of California, Berkeley, California.

John F. Neylan Manuscripts, Bancroft Library, University of California, Berkeley, California.

James D. Phelan Manuscripts, Bancroft Library, University of California, Berkeley, California.

Charles A. Ramm Manuscripts, Archives of the University of California, Berkeley, California.

Chester Rowell Manuscripts, Bancroft Library, University of California, Berkeley, California.

F. S. Stratton Manuscripts, Bancroft Library, University of California, Berkeley, California.

Benjamin I. Wheeler Manuscripts, Archives of the University of California, Berkeley, California.

Peter C. Yorke Manuscripts, Archives of the University of California, Berkeley, California.

Peter C. Yorke Manuscripts, Gleeson Library, University of San Francisco, San Francisco, California.

Consular Dispatches, Hong Kong, 1882-1884. Department of State, General Records, Record Group 59. National Archives, Washington, D.C.

Notes from the Chinese Legation, 1868-1906. Department of State, General Records, Record Group 59. National Archives, Washington, D.C.

PUBLIC DOCUMENTS

United States Census Office, Twelfth Census of the United States, 1900. Washington: 1901.

United States Department of Commerce, Bureau of the Census, Religious Bodies, 1916, Washington: 1910.

The Journal of the Senate, Legislature of the State of California, 35th sess., 16, 320, 344-5, 1293.

INSTITUTIONAL RECORDS

Regents of the University of California, Minute Book, 1900-1912, XIII-XVII. Office of the Secretary of the Regents of the University of California, Berkeley, California.

Regents of the University of California, Committee on Finance. Committee Records, April 20, 1905, VIII. Office of the Secretary of the Regents of the University of California, Berkeley, California.

Regents of the University of California, Committee on Lick Observatory, Committee Records, Sept. 25, 1888, to -.S.15, B.18. Office of the Secretary of the Regents of the University of California, Berkeley, California.

UNPUBLISHED THESIS

Fitzmaurice, Mary C. Historical Development of the Educational Thought of the Reverend Peter C. Yorke, 1893-1925. Unpublished M.A. thesis. University of San Francisco, 1963.

Gaffey, James P. The Life of Patrick William Riordan: Second Archbishop of San Francisco, 1841-1914. Unpublished Ph.D. dissertation. Catholic University of America, 1965.

Kunth, Priscilla F. Nativism in California. Unpublished M.A. thesis. University of California, Berkeley, 1947.

Long, James H. A Factual Study of the Influence of Reverend P. C. Yorke on Education. Unpublished M.A. thesis. Catholic University of America, 1932.

Manion, Mary C. Principles of Catechetic Instruction According to Reverend Peter C. Yorke, Unpublished M.A. thesis. Dominican College, 1953.

BOOKS AND ARTICLES

Barry, E. F. Beautiful Berkeley, Berkeley: Youngs and Barry, 1904.

Bean, Walton. Boss Ruef's San Francisco: The Story of the Union Labor Party, Big Business, and the Graft Prosecution. Berkeley: University of California, 1952.

Benson, Lee. The Concept of Jacksonian Democracy. New York, Atheneum, 1964.

Billington, Ray Allen. The Protestant Crusade, 1800-1860. Chicago: Quadrangle, 1964.

Brusher, Joseph S. "Peter C. Yorke and the A.P.A. in San Francisco," The Catholic Historical Review, XXXVII (July, 1951), 129-150.

---- "Peter C. Yorke, Educator Ahead of His Time," The Catholic Educational Review, XLIV (Feb., 1966), 106-19.

Carter, Everett. "Cultural History Written with Lightning: The Significance of The Birth of a Nation," American Quarterly, XII (Fall, 1960), 347-57.

Cash, W. J. The Mind of the South. New York: Vintage, 1941.

Caughey, John W. California, 2nd ed. Englewood Cliffs: Prentice-Hall, 1960.

Considine, John L. "Father Yorke: Champion of Human Rights," The Ave Maria," (Feb. 18, 1950), 200-8.

Cronin, Bernard C. Father Yorke and the Labor Movement in San Francisco, 1900-1912. Washington, D.C.: Catholic University of America, 1943.

---- "Yorke, Peter Christopher," New Catholic Encyclopedia, XIV (1967), 1075.

Cuddy, Edward. "Pro-Germanism and American Catholicism, 1914-1917," The Catholic

Historical Review, LIV (Oct., 1968), 427-454.

Deutsch, Monroe E., ed. The Abundant Life. Berkeley: University of California, 1926.

Elkins, Stanley M. Slavery: A Problem in American Institutional and Intellectual Life. Universal Library ed., New York: Grosset & Dunlap, 1963.

Ellis, John Tracy. American Catholicism. Chicago: University of Chicago, 1956.

----- American Catholics and the Intellectual Life. Chicago: Heritage Foundation, 1956.

----- ed. Documents of American Catholic History, Milwaukee: Bruce, 1963.

----- The Life of James Cardinal Gibbons: Archbishop of Baltimore, 1834-1921. Milwaukee: Bruce, 1952. 2 vls.

Ferrier, William W. Henry Durant, First President University of California: The New Englander Who Came to California With College on the Brain. Berkeley: private, 1942.

---- Origin and Development of the University of California. Berkeley: Sather Gate Book Shop, 1930.

Handlin, Oscar. Al Smith and His America. Boston: Little, Brown, 1956.

Harris, Arthur. City Manager Government in Berkeley. No. Sp. 18. Chicago: Public Administration Service, 1940.

Hassenger, Robert, ed. The Shape of Catholic Higher Education. Chicago: University of Chicago, 1967.

Hays, Samuel P. "The Politics of Reform in Municipal Government in the Progressive Era," Pacific Northwest Quarterly, 55 (Oct., 1964), 157-169.

Herlihy, David J. "Battle Against Bigotry: Father Peter C. Yorke and the American Protective Association in San Francisco, 1893-1897," Records of the American Catholic Historical Society of Philadelphia, LXII (June, 1951), 95-120.

Herring, Hubert. A History of Latin America, 2d ed. rev. New York: Knopf, 1964.

Higham, John. Strangers in the Land: Patterns of American Nativism, 1860-1925. New York: Atheneum, 1965.

Hodghead, Beverly L. "The General Features of the Berkeley Charter," a speech delivered Sept. 21, 1909. Doe Library, University of California, Berkeley, California.

Hofstadter, Richard. Anti-Intellectualism in American Life. New York: Vintage, 1962.

---- The Age of Reform. New York: Vintage, 1960.

Hogan, Peter E. The Catholic University of America, 1896-1903: The Rectorship of Thomas J. Conaty. Washington, D.C.: Catholic University of America, 1949.

Jones, William Carey. Illustrated History of the University of California, rev. ed. Berkeley: Student's Cooperative Society, 1901.

Joyce, P. J. "Memories of Father Yorke," The Furrow, 2 (Dec., 1951), 688-97.

Knight, Robert E. L. Industrial Relations in the San Francisco Bay Area, 1900-1918. Berkeley: University of California, 1960.

Kurtz, Benjamin P. Charles Mills Gayley. Berkeley: University of California, 1943.

Lemisch, L. Jesse, ed. Benjamin Franklin: The Authobiography and Other Writings. New York: New American Library, 1961.

Leo. "Father Yorke in the Pulpit," The Moraga Quarterly, II (Fall, 1931), 30-40.

Levine, Edward M. The Irish and Irish Politicians: A Study of Cultural and Social Alienation. Notre Dame: University of Notre Dame, 1966.

Lincoln, A. "Roosevelt and Muir at Yosemite," Pacific Discovery, XVI (Jan.-Feb., 1963), 18-22.

McDevitt, Matthew, The Early Years of St. Mary's College (1859-1879). Mimeographed, undated, Distributed through St. Mary's College Alumni Association.

McDonald, William E. "The Pious Fund of the Californias," The Catholic Historical Review, XIX (Jan., 1934), 427-436.

McEnerney, Garret W. "Pious Fund of the Californias," The Catholic Encyclopedia, XII (1913), 106-7.

May, Henry F. "The Recovery of American Religious History," The American Historical Review, LXX (Oct., 1964), 79-92.

Melendy, Howard Brett, and Benjamin F. Gilbert. Governors of California: Peter H. Burnett to Edmund G. Brown. Georgetown, Calif.: Talisman, 1965.

Miller, William. "American Historians and the Business Elite," The Journal of Economic History, IX (Nov., 1949), 184-208.

Mowry, George E. The California Progressives. Chicago: Quadrangle, 1963.

Moynihan, Daniel P. "When the Irish Ran New York," The Reporter, 24 (June 8, 1961), 32-34.

Northern California Writers Program of the Work Projects Administration. Berkeley: The First Seventy-Five Years. Berkeley: Gillick Press, 1941.

Phillips, Ulrich B. American Negro Slavery. New York: Appleton, 1918.

Riordon, William L., ed., Plunkitt of Tammany Hall. New York: E. P. Dutton, 1963.

Rogin, Michael. "Progressivism and the California Electorate," The Journal of American History, LV (Sept., 1968), 297-314.

Shannon, William V. The American Irish, rev. ed. New York: Macmillan, 1966.

Shuck, Oscar T. History of the Bench and Bar of California. Los Angeles: Commercial Printing House, 1901.

Sibley, Robert, ed. The Golden Book of California. Berkeley: California Alumni Association, 1937.

Stadtman, Verne A., ed. The Centennial Record of the University of California. Berkeley: University of California, 1967.

Tannenbaum, Frank. Slave and Citizen: The Negro in the Americas. New York: Vintage, 1946.

Trent, James W. Catholics in College -- Religious Commitment and the Intellectual Life. Chicago: University of Chicago, 1967.

Weber, Francis J. "John Tracy Ellis, Historian of American Catholicism," The American Benedictine Review, XVII (Winter, 1966), 467-478.

Wolfinger, Raymond E. "The Development and Persistence of Ethnic Voting," The American Political Science Review, LIX (Dec., 1965, 896-908.

Yorke, Peter C. America and Ireland: An Open Letter to Mr. Garret W. McEnerney. San Francisco: Text Book, 1918.

---- Educational Lectures. San Francisco: Text Book, 1933.

---- Sermons. San Francisco: Text Book, 1931.

NEWSPAPERS

Bee (Sacramento), Dec. 10, 1908.

Bulletin (San Francisco), Dec. 14, 1898.

Call (*San Francisco), Nov. 2, 27, 1898; Mar. 2, 1908.

Chronicle (San Francisco), May 25, 26, 1900; Aug. 4, 1942.

Daily Californian (Berkeley), Mar.-April, 1903; Jan. 1906; Mar.-April 1908; Mar. 19, 1936; Jan. 20, 1941; Mar. 26, Aug. 4, 1942; Aug. 28, 1944; Mar. 15, Oct. 3, 1960; Feb. 6, 1962; Jan. 26, 1967.

Daily Gazette (Berkeley), 1908; Aug. 5, 1942.

Enquirer (Oakland), May 26, 1900.

Examiner (San Francisco), Nov. 1, 1898; May 1-26, 1900; Aug. 5, 1942.

Leader (San Francisco), Jan. 11, 1902-1904; April 28, 1906; May 12, 1906-July 27, 1912; July 19, 1941.

Monitor (San Francisco), June 2, 16, 1900; Dec. 28, 1951.